Business Intelligence Strategy

A Practical Guide for Achieving BI Excellence

John Boyer

Bill Frank

Brian Green

Tracy Harris

Kay Van De Vanter

MC PRESS

MC Press Online, LLC

Ketchum, ID 83340

Business Intelligence Strategy
A Practical Guide for Achieving BI Excellence
John Boyer, Bill Frank, Brian Green, Tracy Harris, Kay Van De Vanter

First Edition
Third Printing—December 2011

MC Press offers excellent discounts on this book when ordered in quantity for bulk purchases or special sales, which may include custom covers and content particular to your business, training goals, marketing focus, and branding interest.

MC Press Online, LLC
    Corporate Offices
    P.O. Box 4886
    Ketchum, ID 83340-4886 USA
For information regarding sales and/or customer service, please contact:
    MC Press
    P.O. Box 4300
    Big Sandy, TX 75755-4300 USA
    Toll Free: 1-877-226-5394
For information regarding permissions or special orders, please contact:
    mcbooks@mcpressonline.com

ISBN: 978-158347-362-7

Acknowledgements

We would all like to thank the IBM team and their extensive list of subject-matter experts who contributed content, joined our discussions, and helped to provide expertise that was critical to making this book possible: Thank you to Michael Dziekan and Forrest Palmer, who spent many hours with our team providing their deep expertise and guidance and contributing significant content and graphics, particularly on organizational structures and competency centers. And to Meg Dussault, who helped enlighten our team to the "sweet spots" of information. Thank you to Kevin Cohen and Derek Lacks for their assistance with and debates on the many levels of value within an organization. And to Andreas Coucopoulos, for his many hours delving into the technology strategy that is so critical to a strategic initiative. We would also like to thank Rob Ashe, Eric Yau, Harriet Fryman, and Mychelle Mollot for their support in making this book possible.

We also want to thank the MC Press team—Merrikay Lee, Victoria Mack, Thomas Stockwell, and Katie Tipton—for their patience and expertise, as well as Susan Visser from the IBM Information Management team at IBM.

From John Boyer

I would like to thank my chain of management—Oussama Warwar, Jeff Henry, and Dirk Izzo—who contributed to the content and helped me understand how the corporate vision is translated to strategy. I am also deeply indebted to the BICoE Team—Mangai, Robert, Ram, Venkat, Guru, and KT—who make my job easy. You put the "E" in the BICoE. Thank you, too, to Lynn Moore; best of luck on your book, my friend.

From Bill Frank

I would like to thank all of the IBM Cognos team who made themselves available in our BI journey over the years, the Cognos Innovation Center, Tracy Harris, and the "cheese kids." There are so many individuals from J&J that have been my sounding board, taken initiative to turn ideas into reality, shaped my thinking, collaborated with me, and put up with my endless evangelizing about standards, practices, and the need for a BICC. I'm sure I'd miss someone in the short space I have here if I started listing names. I would like to thank the SSB BI Domain, the BITS team, the BICC leads, and the entire J&J BI COP for their efforts that have led to successes in transforming, improving, and creating innovation with BI solutions across the enterprise. Thanks also to the members of my immediate management as well as senior executives who have encouraged, mentored, and supported me.

From Brian Green

On behalf of BlueCross BlueShield of Tennessee, I would like to acknowledge the dedication and contributions of the entire Data Management and Information Delivery team. I would also like to acknowledge Frank Brooks for his tremendous leadership, vision, and support. Thanks also to the members of my immediate management as well as senior executives who have encouraged, mentored, and supported me.

From Tracy Harris

A big thanks to Leah MacMillan, Meg Dussault, and Harriet Fryman for their guidance, insight, and vision and for recognizing the critical need for this endeavor. I would also like to thank Debbie Ng and Jacqueline Coolidge for helping to initially bring this "excellent" group together to make this book possible. Thank you also to Jennifer Schmitz, Becky Smith, Jennifer Hanniman, Rebecca Wormleighton, Brent Winsor, Catherine Frye, and Nina Sandy for their significant contributions to this endeavor.

From Kay Van De Vanter

I would like to thank my fellow Boeing Business Intelligence Competency Center team members and management for their insightful comments and discussions. Special thanks to our BICC executive manager for his careful reviews and attention to detail and to our communications focal for working closely with me to obtain the permissions and approvals needed to participate in this endeavor.

Finally, we would like to thank the various thought leaders and analysts in the industry who continue to provide critical research in this area that allows organizations to better understand how they can achieve success. In particular, we would like to acknowledge the teams at BIScorecard, Nucleus Research, Business Applications Research Center, Gartner, Forrester, and TDWI. And we would like to thank Roland Mosimann, Patrick Mosimann, and Jack Musgrove at BII, PMSI, and Aline for their research, support, vision, and foundational contributions to this effort.

About the Authors

The content for this book was prepared by the IBM Cognos BI Excellence Advisory Board, a team of representatives from leading enterprise organizations who research, advise, and share best practices for achieving excellence in Business Intelligence and Performance Management initiatives.

John Boyer

John Boyer is manager of the BI Advisory Team at The Nielsen Company. There, he oversees adoption, enablement, and internal consulting for all things BI. Before joining Nielsen, John spent several years as a BI architect and trusted advisor at IBM. After graduating from medical school, his aptitude, passion, and bedside manner took him first to a healthcare clinic, where he rose to Director of Finance and Information Systems. John has spent the past 15 years consulting in software development, business intelligence, and data warehousing.

John is chair of the Illinois Cognos User Group. As a conference speaker, he has been invited to speak at a number of national events, including Information on Demand, Cognos Forum, and the Composite Software User Group.

About The Nielsen Company

The Nielsen Company (*www.nielsen.com*) is a leading global information and media company providing essential integrated marketing and media measurement information, analytics, and industry expertise to clients around the world. Through its broad portfolio of products and services, Nielsen tracks sales of consumer products, reports on television viewing habits in countries representing more than 60 percent of the world's population, and measures Internet audiences. Nielsen also produces trade shows, print publications, and online newsletters. The company is active in approximately 100 countries, with headquarters in New York City.

Bill Frank

Bill Frank is the Manager, ITGF BI Practice, at Johnson & Johnson. He has more than 25 years of experience in decision support and business intelligence and is a certified Project Management Professional (PMP). Bill has worked in several major companies, including AT&T, Time Warner, and most recently Johnson & Johnson. At J&J, Bill has played a key role in the development of BI solutions, organizational model, governance, and practices and in evangelizing BI across the enterprise. Bill is a founding member of the J&J BI Center of Practice and co-leads this 300-member internal group focused on leverage, communication, and sharing proven practices.

Bill also serves as the liaison to the IBM Cognos executive, marketing, and technology teams. He teamed with other J&J teams to lead the creation of the IBM Cognos enterprise agreement and the shared environments that are key to supporting J&J's standardization and consolidation efforts. Currently, Bill is developing enterprise data warehouse and BI strategies to support the J&J Global Finance organization. He is also a member of the IBM BI Excellence Advisory Board and several other external organizations focused on BI technologies.

About Johnson & Johnson

Johnson & Johnson (*www.jnj.com*) is a Fortune 100™ company, encompassing the world's premier consumer health company, the world's largest and most diverse medical devices and diagnostics company, fourth-largest biologics company, and eighth-largest pharmaceuticals company. J&J has more than 250 operating companies in 60 countries and employs approximately 114,000 people. The company is headquartered in New Brunswick, New Jersey.

Brian Green

Brian Green is Manager of Business Intelligence and Performance Management at BlueCross BlueShield of Tennessee. He has 30 years of information management experience in the insurance industry, with expertise in process improvement and organizational development to align delivery of solutions with business strategy.

About BlueCross BlueShield of Tennessee

BlueCross BlueShield of Tennessee (*www.bcbst.com*) offers its clients peace of mind through affordable solutions for health and healing, life and living. Founded in 1945, the Chattanooga, Tennessee-based company is focused on reinventing the health plan for its three million members. Through its integrated health management approach, BlueCross develops patient-centric products and services that positively impact affordability, patient safety, and quality. BlueCross BlueShield of Tennessee, Inc., is an independent licensee of the BlueCross BlueShield Association.

Tracy Harris

Tracy Harris is Senior Manager, BI Excellence, at IBM. She is responsible for chairing the BI Excellence Advisory Board and managing the BI Excellence Program and Champion initiative at IBM. These programs are designed to help organizations achieve success, business value, and excellence in their BI and performance management initiatives and are defined through the sharing of best practices, research, and guidance from industry leaders and subject-matter experts. Tracy has worked with Fortune 500® organizations and government organizations around the globe to gather and research best practices in achieving excellence, and she shares this research through workshops and speaking engagements worldwide on the topic.

About IBM

International Business Machines Corporation (*www.ibm.com*) is one of the world's largest technology companies—a multinational computer, technology, and IT consulting corporation headquartered in Armonk, New York. IBM manufactures and sells computer hardware and software and offers infrastructure services, hosting services, and consulting services in areas ranging from mainframe computers to nanotechnology. With nearly 400,000 employees worldwide and sales of more than 100 billion U.S. dollars, IBM holds more patents than any other U.S. technology company and operates eight research laboratories worldwide. The company has scientists, engineers, consultants, and sales professionals in over 200 countries. IBM employees have earned five Nobel Prizes, four Turing Awards, nine National Medals of Technology, and five National Medals of Science.

Kay Van De Vanter

Kay Van De Vanter is an information management domain architect and enterprise BI architect for The Boeing Company, with more than 12 years of experience in IT and business intelligence areas. For the past seven years, she has led Boeing's Business Intelligence Competency Center team and has worked with several other key information management teams to drive the standardization and alignment of BI initiatives at Boeing. Kay has also collaborated with industry BI professionals, user groups, and teams to help drive innovation and quality in the BI tools used by Boeing. She is currently partnering with others to develop an enterprise BI and technology strategy in support of Boeing's business goals. Kay is a member of IBM's BI Excellence Advisory Board and BI Customer Advisory Board, as well as other external user groups focused on BI technologies and best practices.

About The Boeing Company

The Boeing Company (*www.boeing.com*) is the world's largest aerospace company and leading manufacturer of commercial jetliners and defense, space, and security systems. Boeing products and tailored services include commercial and military aircraft, satellites, weapons, electronic and defense systems, launch systems, advanced information and communications systems, and performance-based logistics and training. Boeing's Engineering, Operations, and Technology business unit supports the company's business units by delivering high-quality, low-cost technical services in IT, research and technology, and test and evaluation; integrated enterprise strategies that ensure technology is ready when needed, competitively protected, and environmentally progressive; and disciplined and efficient engineering, operations, and supplier management support that ensures program success.

Contents

Preface

Business Intelligence Strategy: A Practical Guide for Achieving BI Excellence has been a project in the making for more than two years. The book began as a series of BI Excellence Advisory Board monthly roundtables. These discussions evolved to a number of white papers that were developed with Advisory Board members, subject-matter experts from IBM, and various thought leaders in the industry. This content was then compiled into the IBM BI Champion Kit and finally into the book you are reading today.

The BI Excellence Advisory Board was established by IBM in 2008. Made up of a group of experts in the business intelligence field across several different industries, the Advisory Board was born out a recognition that although BI was an important technology for many organizations, it appeared that for many, success was limited. With this realization in mind, IBM brought leaders from well-known, highly successful BI programs together to discuss how they achieved success. Each of these professionals was a recognized, practicing leader in the BI industry. Each had enabled thousands of users in their organizations, had large-scale BI departments or BI communities, and had successfully created standard people, process, and technology programs in the BI practice in their organizations. They had significantly reduced costs for their companies, increased efficiencies, and reduced time for many of their important processes. IBM brought these experts together as an Advisory Board to discuss common challenges these leaders encountered in their journeys and determine proven ways in which those challenges were overcome.

This group of individual organizations met on a regular basis, tackling various topics with each and every meeting. Each member had slightly different areas of expertise that he or she could lend to the discussions:

- John Boyer managed the BI Center of Excellence at Nielsen.

- Bill Frank at Johnson & Johnson focused on BI solutions for finance, internally evangelized BI concepts and technologies, and co-led the company's 300-member BI Community of Practice.

- Brian Green was part of the overall information management division at BlueCross BlueShield of Tennessee and managed the company's BI and Performance Management areas.

- Tracy Harris was part of IBM's Business Analytics division, researching best practices in achieving excellence and chairing the IBM BI Excellence Advisory Board.

- Kay Van De Vanter was the lead BI Architect in the Boeing IT BICC.

Over months of discussion, several subject-matter experts were brought in, and a few contributed significantly to this group and to the content of the book, including Michael Dziekan, who provided deep expertise on the chapters related to organizational structures; Forrest Palmer, who shared his knowledge of business alignment strategy; and Andreas Coucopoulos, who lent valuable insights on technology strategy—all from the IBM team. Several topics were tackled, including user adoption, executive buy-in, and organizational structures, and each of these topics was found to have been a common challenge for every member of the group, regardless of industry. This exploration led to a series of white papers, developed through these conversations by IBM, on the best practices to overcome these challenges. The content of these papers formed a strong backbone upon which we expanded for the book, and many of these papers contributed directly to the content.

As the meetings unfolded, a set of distinct common challenges was identified as the main cause for the typical issues encountered in organizations. Each of these challenges impacted one another and caused the various symptoms that existed. The preparation of white papers led to further development of a Web site—the BI Champion's Kit—that tackled each of these initiatives.

The group continued to meet and determined that in order to truly be successful, it was not only a technology strategy that was important to a BI program but also a business alignment strategy and an organizational and behavioral strategy that were implemented as part of their success.

This book discusses a BI strategy, but it also recognizes that a BI platform—what you might think of as reporting, analysis, dashboard, and scorecard capabilities—enables and supports a broader set of capabilities, such as financial planning, budgeting, forecasting, realtime monitoring, and advanced analytics, that are also impacted by other technologies and programs: data warehousing, quality, integration, governance, and others. This means that in the BI strategy, these other technologies and stakeholders have to be consulted, supported, or enabled in the process.

The book also recognizes the value of an agile BI methodology. An organization is not going to implement a two-year project and go into lockdown for that length of time. Nor is the expectation that a strategy is prepared once and will last the lifetime of the BI program. A BI strategy is meant to change—it needs to deliver a series of wins over time. It is meant to be evaluated on a regular basis, and the standards that are chosen are also evaluated and tested over time.

However, creating a BI strategy also requires a collaborative approach across an organization, which means putting standard processes, technologies, and roles in place. It is recognized that the standards don't necessarily change each time a new technology is delivered—because you know there will be new technologies on the horizon—but they are evaluated with business partners, vendors are asked for their roadmaps, and business and IT work together to deliver an approach that will best suit the needs of the organization. There are many situations where, given regulations, chaotic spreadsheets and tools that lack consistency and security are not acceptable. And there are definite controls that need to be put on information in many cases.

All of the represented organizations realize that they have not successfully completed their BI journey—far from it—but have embarked on a journey to BI excellence that has led to wins and enabled foundational elements to be put in place. And all continue to learn and tweak their plans. It is a journey for the long term and a journey that will change over time and deliver success and competitiveness for the organizations into the future. Improvements are continual, and each organization looks forward to future innovations and change, but each has also realized the mission-critical value that a strategic BI program provides. These organizations have embarked on a journey in which they can truly link strategy to execution through the leverage of technologies that enable success in this area.

We hope you enjoy reading this guide as you prepare for your own journey to BI excellence. It is meant to deliver a framework by which you can prepare your unique strategy, and it provides a practical discussion of suggested strategies, tactical tips, and proven practices that the authors have learned in their BI excellence journey. As you make that trek down the road to success and encounter challenges along the way, know that you are not alone. Please join our community by visiting the IBM BI Champion Kit (*www.ibm.com/cognos/champion*) and telling us about your journey.

The IBM BI Excellence Advisory Board
John, Bill, Brian, Tracy, and Kay
September 2010

Introduction

According to the 2009 IBM Global CIO study, BI and analytics is the number one priority for chief information officers (CIOs)[1]. Business and IT leaders alike understand that these technologies will provide the best opportunity to gain insight and decision-making capabilities that can help organizations uncover new opportunities, increase efficiencies, and reach corporate goals.

Yet many organizations are struggling to implement strategic BI initiatives that can help improve enterprise-level access to the information needed to support business improvement. After decades of building the information infra-structure and amassing oceans of data, it seems many organizations have found themselves with silos of knowledge that are difficult to reconcile, complex to comprehend, and limited in their ability to provide the needed insight.

- According to a *Computerworld* survey, only 14 percent of organizations are connecting strategy to execution with these technologies.[2]

- In the same study, 67 percent of these organizations claim that there is a lack of time, resources, and budget applied to these efforts.

- And, according to a TDWI research report, user adoption is at only 24 percent for these initiatives.[3]

Why is there such a discrepancy between the needs of business and the ability to meet these needs with business intelligence (BI) initiatives? If BI is truly the top priority, how is it possible that there are budget or resource issues? Why, in corporations that have begun to implement BI, are user adoption levels so low? How can business intelligence be the number one priority, and yet so few can claim success?

We believe the reasons are often because many implementations are treated solely as a technology initiative—but the challenges exist beyond the technology. Many issues, in fact, are non-technical in nature and may not be addressed as a BI program is rolled out. In our discussions with various professionals in organizations around the globe, we have determined that many of the biggest hurdles over time were likely due to the following issues:

- There was no *strategy* in place—and if you don't know what you're trying to achieve, you will never get there.

- There were no *metrics to define or measure success*, no business case for the endeavor, and no demonstrated justification of the value.

- *Politics and culture* derailed the project easily with a lack of executive buy-in, low user adoption, and an inability to create change.

- There was no *organizational structure for BI* in place, with a strong emphasis on communication, to offer the skills, manage the program, and provide the needed momentum.

- The solutions that have been attempted are *piecemeal*, disconnected, and costly to maintain without delivering the confidence in the information that is needed or the promised return on investment.

In other words, the obstacles to a successful BI implementation are not solely technological in nature; in fact, they are often societal within the organization itself. The result is that a BI initiative can easily be derailed by these factors, producing less value due to inconsistent behavior and thereby losing momentum in an organization. The projects that succeed are most often the result of a successful combination of people, process, and technology strategies because it is difficult to have a successful technology endeavor when the other ingredients are not present.

The Business Value of Successful Business Intelligence

So why would an organization endeavor to implement a strategic business intelligence program? It appears that there are, in fact, many organizations that have various tactical implementations that are quite successful. Is it not just about using a technology in the areas that are needed?

It is true that a technology should be applied to the areas it can enable. However, most organizations—due to their tactical implementations of BI to date—have not yet realized the mission-critical value that BI can provide to the reaction time, monitoring, and predictive ability that can be found in a successful implementation. The ability to measure and monitor how organizations are executing against corporate goals—to understand whether they are on or off track and why—and the ability to change direction when necessary has not yet been enabled due to the limitations of the current environment.

If we were to compare this situation with other, more mature technologies that are considered mission-critical in today's organizations—let's take e-mail, for example—would it be efficient, productive, and cost-effective to have pockets of employees on a variety of different e-mail systems, some of which might not integrate or communicate effectively with others? How would this situation impact the productivity of an organization's work force?

Consider a customer view: if the information is siloed across various departments, how can a consistent view be understood and accessed to provide the best possible service to the party in question with tactical silos of information? Is it productive to manually pull together this information? Is it accurate? Efficient?

We believe that a strategic, enterprise business intelligence program offers higher value to our companies, especially in today's fast-paced, changing environment.

- First, it can reduce the total cost of ownership (TCO) for IT and increase the return on investment (ROI) for software and hardware. It also increases the amount of time IT can spend on strategic work rather than duplicate manual labor. This creates increased IT efficiency.

- Second, it can leverage the IT infrastructure and a set of skills to give business users direct access to enterprise-wide information so they can make critical decisions. This increases the company's overall productivity and business efficiency.

- Last, and best of all, a successful BI program can increase collaboration and leverage the decision-support structure across the enterprise to increase overall business effectiveness. This includes a better utilization of resources, a critical consistent view of reliable data across the entire corporation, and the implementation of metrics to measure the progress of key decision areas. Indeed, a successful BI program can provide executives with the visibility they need into the performance drivers that propel the business forward.

However, in most cases, organizations tend to focus on only the IT efficiencies that the BI technology can provide, resulting in a continued value justification exercise and a difficult time in providing a business case. If we consider the business value hierarchy offered in the book The *Performance Manager*[4] and depicted in Figure I.1, we can see that the three levels of value are not all of equal worth. And as you move up the value scale, they become more difficult to measure—especially if business and IT alignment is not strong.

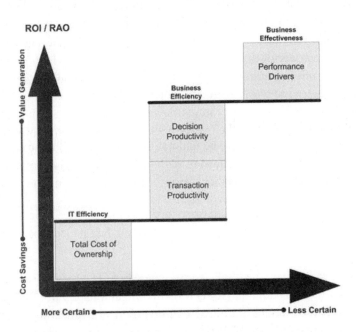

Figure I.1: The business value hierarchy for measuring ROI.[5]

However, to achieve excellence, an organization needs to deliver value in all three areas and must learn to partner with the right stakeholders to do so effectively.

Getting to this level of a strategic BI program is not an overnight endeavor. It may have taken years, generations, or even a century to implement the array of different technologies and data silos that likely exist in an organization. Therefore, it is understood that turning this data into information that provides decision-making capabilities and results will also require time, resources, and effort. This is an effort that should not be done in isolation over a long time period until perfection is achieved. It is an effort that needs to occur in a series of smaller successes, in an agile methodology—to ensure continued momentum is achieved. It needs to reflect the needs of the company today and tomorrow. It needs to change over time as the organization changes. Most important—to achieve this type of change—it is one that requires deep collaboration between IT and the various business community members that are stakeholders to achieve meaningful results.

This is a process that each of our organizations has been undertaking over a number of years, and one that will continue to evolve and change over time. Each of our programs has encountered challenges along the way, and we have come together to share these challenges and offer insight into how successful initiatives have been created.

In this effort, we have discovered that there is a common ground for our successes. Successful programs were implemented not just with a technology strategy in mind but also with the involvement of the community of stakeholders. Getting that critical buy-in ensured that corporate goals, people, and processes were also taken into account. With this discovery, we have created a strategy framework for a strategic BI program that can be used to accelerate an organization's success in this initiative. We call this the BI Excellence Strategy Framework.

The BI Excellence Strategy Framework

The BI Excellence Strategy Framework can be used as a guide for organizations in any industry to help create a BI strategy. This strategy will ensure that the variety of elements that can derail an initiative or improve success are considered. It extends far beyond technology, factoring in people and process as key elements of success. The framework is a practical guide to creating your strategy, ensuring your effort aligns to corporate goals in a pragmatic way. It helps you to deliver agility in the implementation that will maintain momentum, and it recognizes the political and cultural challenges that can be overcome before they happen. In this book, we take you through the strategy framework and also offer practical advice and proven practices that we have learned along the way—as well as tactics you can use as you move forward in your endeavor.

What this framework will do is provide a practical guide to help an organization understand many of the considerations it needs to include in a strategy. What it will not do is provide you with a ready-made strategy. The framework recognizes that each organization is different; culture, structure, maturity level, and strategy will all affect a BI program, and each of these needs to be part of the well-thought-out plan to ensure success.

What the framework also will not do is give you a strategy that starts today and ends after a set period of time, when results can be claimed and the initiative can be considered over. A BI program is a journey—an ongoing effort that should, in fact, change over time, should be measured regularly against established benchmarks, and should be flexible enough to change. It should also be reviewed on a regular basis, tweaked, and realigned to ensure it is meeting the needs of the business.

Consider Your Level of Maturity

Where is your organization on the BI maturity scale? Let's measure ourselves against a very simple framework for typical BI initiatives (Figure I.2). If stage 1 is at the lower scale of a BI program maturity level and stage 4 is the highest level of maturity, where would you place your organization?

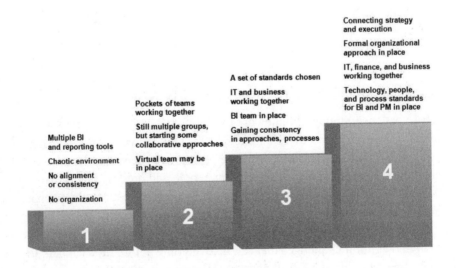

Figure I.2: BI maturity levels.

Level of maturity will also affect your strategy, and you need to consider this as you create your strategy. Your maturity level will change as your organization matures, causing elements of the strategy to change over time. You will therefore need to revisit your strategy on a regular basis.

You will need to strive for each incremental step—not jump from stage 1 to 4 today. You will need to adjust each level of your strategy to reflect these changes—while measuring the changes in the program to determine success.

Business Intelligence Excellence

So, what is BI excellence anyway? We believe that business intelligence excellence is achieved when organizations have in place the strategy, people, process, and technology approaches that result in business impact, value, and effectiveness. Value and business impact are best achieved when the use of BI, performance management (PM), and analytics spans departments and silos to provide an enterprise view of information and a collaborative team approach to organizationally achieving goals. This requires a defined approach that takes into account:

- Business strategy alignment, vision, and business case
- Cultural and organizational behavior
- Technology and tools strategy

Therefore, to achieve excellence, these three elements need to be considered in the initial plan.

Furthermore, each element of the framework relies upon an active, mutual relationship between business users and the IT team. Each element of the strategy also provides a high contribution to each value driver level in the business value hierarchy. It is not necessarily just a one-to-one relationship, but each area definitely aligns closely to the three areas of the business value hierarchy. To achieve the highest levels of value, all three strategy elements must be considered—and doing so will result in increased success for the BI program overall (Figure I.3).

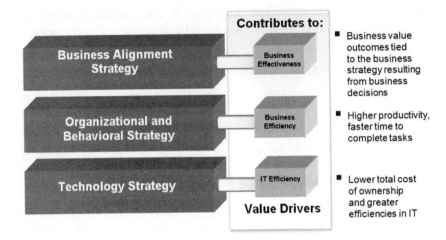

Figure I.3: Achieving the highest levels of value.

Strategies for Success

This book is divided into three critical sections, each associated with one of the key strategies of the framework. It provides the higher-level overview of what each strategy needs to contain and includes tactics and proven practices that we have used in our organizations in each of these areas. The experiences of our team in building these strategies within our separate corporations are condensed and offered as guidelines and observations. Let's examine each strategic element quickly before delving into the details.

The Business Alignment Strategy

Our organizations are leaders in their respective market sectors, and we believe that our ability to get insight and visibility into the information that matters is indeed one of the strong enablers of our success. These systems help to enable our teams to discover new opportunities, improve processes, and make better, more informed decisions while reducing overall operational costs.

However, before any organization can begin to provide its employees with the tools needed to deliver on the promise of BI, it needs to ensure that it measures what matters. It has to define the metrics that need to be measured, align them to corporate priorities, and understand who the users of this information are and how they intend to use it. A partnership between those on the business side—who can help define the sweet spots—and those who know the data is critical.

But how do you align business goals and the data that exists in an organization? And how do you reconcile top-down strategies with bottom-up implementations? That's the terrain we traverse in our first critical chapter. We'll talk about:

- Assessing your current situation

- Strategic management approaches

- Mapping corporate objectives to bottom-up needs

- Constructing a methodology toward performance management

- Defining the business case

This area of the strategy is about leveraging the knowledge and guidance of the key business stakeholders and creating a collaborative partnership with those who know the data to create a roadmap of wins that create success and maintain momentum.

The Organizational and Cultural Strategy

In our second chapter, we examine the cultural mechanisms within the organization that can create challenges for even the most solid BI programs. How do you manage politics and culture within an organization? How do you prepare for organizational readiness in support of a strategic initiative?

As our organizations have grown and matured, we, too, have often found pockets of resistance to the changes that a comprehensive BI program requires. Users are often already content with the tools and processes they're using. Their day-to-day activities can appear divorced from the understanding of the larger needs of the organization. When change is required, obstruction and resistance are often the result of a lack of understanding of the goals. How do you manage change in these instances?

The organizational and cultural strategy area of the framework takes on that challenge. We start with the business goals identified by the business alignment strategy and then use a variety of techniques to win the support from users and line-of-business managers. We offer proven practices for organizational readiness, such as the establishment of a BI Center of Competency or Excellence. We talk about the keys to keeping a program on track, such as winning the support of users through collaboration, training, and a continuous communication process.

In this chapter, we'll talk, among many things, about:

- Understanding your business culture and communicating the goals of the program

- How to obtain executive support and how to leverage that support for the benefit of the project

- The value of an organizational structure or a BI Competency Center with potential organizational design approaches and funding models

- The challenges of gaining user adoption of the technology

- Showcasing your program to maintain momentum

By considering the many organizational and behavioral factors that can derail an initiative, you can plan and prepare early, increase communication and buy-in, and design an aligned approach that will help initiate change in an organization.

The Technology Strategy

While we noted earlier that many of the challenges facing enterprise BI programs are not specifically related to the technology, we do recognize that a solid technology strategy that meets the needs of the business is critical to success. This tends to be the area that most organizations focus on in developing a strong design plan, but we believe it is only one of three areas that requires consideration. We believe that the technology strategy needs to be defined in alignment with the business and with an understanding of the needs of the various stakeholders, not just to meet the needs of IT.

Our organizations have made major investments in information technologies, including CRM, ERP, and a slew of other transactional systems that run the operations of our divisions and subsidiaries. IT and business have also invested in numerous BI tools at divisional levels. We also know that the premise of a "one size fits all" solution is both financially and operationally impractical. So, how do we devise the technology strategy that will leverage what we have, position the infrastructure for growth, and meet the requirements that our business alignment strategy promises—all while improving our total cost of ownership?

That's the subject matter of Chapter 3: building the technology strategy that can support the requirements of an enterprise-level BI program. In this chapter, we will discuss:

- Standardization and consolidation (what it means and how it can be done effectively and realistically)

- Improving the total cost of ownership and leveraging existing investments

- Delivering the multiple capabilities and an information platform that will enable an enterprise

- Information and technology governance

- Delivering confidence in the information

- Deployment options

The array of technologies that surround, support, and are enabled by business intelligence are broad and vast, and in this chapter we aim to provide an overview of which technologies you need to consider in your strategy and which stakeholders you need to bring on board.

Building Excellence in BI and PM

In managing and building our BI programs, we agree with *The Performance Manager* principle that companies should be able to answer three key questions:

- How are we doing?

- Why?

- What should we be doing?

These may seem like common-sense questions to ask, but too many companies have found that they're extremely difficult questions to answer.

We believe our BI platform enables an array of technologies in our organization and needs to be strongly supported by others. Our companies should be able to measure and monitor key metrics using scorecards and dashboards and to draw reports and analyze data to gain context, understand trends, predict future outcomes, and spot anomalies. And we believe our companies should be able to model future scenarios using the planning, budgeting, and forecasting tools that can spell the difference between business success and business failure.

Although our work is far from finished, we believe our BI Excellence Framework is the foundation of our ongoing success in defining, managing, and supporting our BI programs. We offer this framework to you in the hope that it brings your organization similar benefits in the months and years ahead.

This book was initiated because we recognized that all organizations face many of these challenges. They are real challenges, but ones that can be overcome. You are not alone—these challenges are common, and many are, in fact, due to human nature. This book offers you some practical guidance to address these common challenges while providing food for thought and setting you on your way to defining your own strategy for success.

Chapter 1

Defining Your
Business Alignment Strategy

W hat strategic approach do top-performing, breakaway organizations share? According to the IBM Institute for Business Value study *Breaking Away with Business Analytics and Optimization*, it is the use of business intelligence and analytics. Using BI, analytics, and performance management eliminates information overload by making sense of the massive amount of information that is now available in the enterprise. In order to become a breakaway organization, companies need to establish both a vision about the strategic use of information and a plan to implement this vision.[1]

We know that most organizations have an understanding of one or more of the basic elements of corporate business strategy. They typically define, at least on an annual basis, their top corporate objectives and business unit strategies. They analyze their markets, determine their direction, and create a plan to ensure that resources are available and stakeholders informed. However, it is apparent that most organizations do not sufficiently link these plans to daily operations or manage execution effectively. And while it is recognized that BI technologies can be an enabler to successful execution, many do not have a business alignment strategy that allows them to plan their strategies via data-driven metrics and BI or to map these corporate objectives in order to effectively monitor results to ensure objectives are achieved. This area is often either overlooked completely or implemented on an ad hoc basis versus as part of the basic success of the business strategy.

In fact, according to a study conducted by IBM in September 2010, only 22 percent of organizations are successfully linking strategy to execution with BI and performance management.[2] And we know that when companies fail in strategy execution, company results can suffer.

On the flip side, however, this means that roughly one in five companies is successful in its strategy execution. Such organizations can reap the benefits of overall performance improvements, gaining competitive advantage, finding new opportunities, and creating business impact that is aligned with their goals. They have enabled visibility into the information that matters and improved decision-making capabilities. With the ability to understand, anticipate, and shape outcomes through innovative technologies, these organizations can help to increase efficiencies and effectiveness throughout the key areas of the organization.

Our task in this chapter is to explore considerations and identify steps in developing an effective business alignment strategy for a strategic business intelligence initiative. It should map to corporate business strategy to enable successful execution, a critical first step in the strategic BI initiative. This includes the following:

1. **Assessing Your Current Situation**—Understanding the corporate strategy and identifying how your organization is currently managing its business strategy and monitoring and measuring outcomes

2. **Developing Effective Strategies for Linking the Business Strategy to BI Initiatives**—Examining strategies that are used today and determining how your organization can develop an effective business alignment strategy that improves outcomes and results

3. **Involving Key Stakeholders and Priority Business Areas**—Understanding how to determine, prioritize, and involve key stakeholders who can influence the business and execution strategies

4. **Implementing Sound Solutions**—Learning how proven practices can transform the effectiveness of the organization

An Introduction to Strategic Management Approaches

So how can strategy be managed to achieve the desired outcomes? Many different strategic management approaches may be in use within the organization.

Organizations use various methods today, and others have been used in the past. As examples, some of the highly common ones include, but are not limited to:

- **Balanced Scorecard (BSC)**—A strategic planning and management system that aligns business activities to the strategy of the organization. BSC offers the following:

  » Stresses the communication of the strategy—both internally and externally—and monitors the progress of the organization against strategic goals

  » Adds strategic non-financial performance measurements to the financial metrics to provide a more balanced view of organizational behavior

  » Applies metrics to the decision-making areas of finance, customer, internal process, and innovation

  BSC became popular in the 1990s and is used today by entrepreneurial firms as well as some government departments.[3]

- **Six Sigma (6S)**—A very rigorous system of management tactics that seeks to improve the quality of *process outputs* by identifying and removing the causes of defects (errors) and minimizing variability in manufacturing and business processes. 6S does the following:

  » Uses a set of quality management methods, including statistical methods

  » Creates a special infrastructure of people within the organization (Black Belts, Green Belts, and so on) who are experts in these methods

  » Follows a defined sequence of steps and has quantified *targets*; these targets can be financial (cost reduction or profit increase) or whatever is critical to the customer of that process (e.g., cycle time, safety, delivery)

  Six Sigma was originally developed by Motorola in 1981 and was used first in manufacturing. Its roots are based heavily on Japanese quality improvement initiatives in the automotive industry. It focuses on quantifiable bottom-line results that are tied to strategy.[4]

- **Total Quality Management (TQM)**—A management concept that is often associated with developing, deploying, and maintaining organizational systems required for various business processes. TQM achieves these goals:

» Reduces the errors produced during the manufacturing or service process

» Increases customer satisfaction

» Streamlines supply-chain management

» Modernizes equipment and ensures workers have the highest level of training

TQM is closely associated with Six Sigma and differs mainly in its approach. W. Edwards Deming is considered the founder of this management model, which preceded Six Sigma.[5]

All of these are solid approaches to managing strategy, and chances are good that management decision-makers use more than one of these, in addition to other management tactics, to control and direct the organization. However, whichever one is used, some common themes arise from these approaches:

- **Goals**—The definition and selection of strategic objectives and/or goals

- **Measurements**—The consolidation of measurement information relevant to an organization's progress against these objectives and goals

- **Indicators and Metrics**—Key Performance Indicators (KPIs) and metrics defined with specific targets and attached to specific objectives

- **Performance**—The interaction and/or interventions made by managers in response to these indicators to apply corrective actions and improve future performance against the goals

Our business alignment strategy process isn't designed to replace any individual approach; rather, it's recommended to orchestrate activities within the organization so that these approaches work together seamlessly. In other words, our process is to help transform *strategy definition* into *strategy execution* using BI, analytics, and performance management.

What do we mean?

In a 2010 survey conducted by IBM, more than 50 percent of organizations indicated that there was a disconnect between what the business needs and what IT delivers.[6] The alignment between these groups can often lead to the inability to work together toward the goals that matter in an organization.

What type of goals matter?

Put simply, the goals that matter most are the ones that are most closely linked to the top corporate objectives. Most often, they are also the goals that tie most directly to revenue and expense management.

Therefore, the key to executing the strategy is to a) *communicate* the strategy across the organization and then b) *act on* new directions identified by the strategy. This can be done using the tactical tools and measurements implemented within the key decision areas to provide visibility and the ability to anticipate and drive future outcomes.

Assessing Your Current Situation

How closely is your organization connecting strategy to execution? What are your company's top objectives? How are they currently executed? How are you measuring and monitoring whether you are on or off track?

As we assess our current environments, it's often easy to see where an organization is aligning business strategies to a BI initiative.

However, as our organizations have grown, separate silos of information have evolved over years or generations. Some of these silos may be viewed as proprietary within an individual department or subsidiary. Some may have been created by processes that are invisible to those outside that area of responsibility or may be based on processes that are no longer current or common.

In order to create a comprehensive business alignment strategy for a strategic BI initiative, collaborative teams need to make progress in revealing these information sources and strategically managing that information to create insight that produces high-value results. The high-value areas important to the business alignment strategy need to be harnessed, and the political cultures representing those organizational entities need to be brought together in a collective to produce results as cross-functional teams rather than individual groups.

The outcomes of a business alignment strategy for business intelligence—the business goals we are we are trying to achieve—will help define how to get there and produce better collaboration across teams to work together to achieve those results. Without a clear vision of the connection to strategy, operating in silos and within communities or cultures is a natural instinct. Though there might be substantial effort and complexities, with good vision that is tied to the practicalities of a given business, a strategy can be created that moves the company from the tactical use of information to a focused organization that uses the information strategically in everyday processes.

Where Do We Start?

If your organization is like many, you likely already have a number of BI initiatives taking place—some successful and many that are producing less value. The key to transforming these multiple projects into a high-value strategic initiative is to assess which ones are successful, why they are successful, and how they connect to priority objectives. You can then use this information to create a business alignment strategy for BI and analytics that will define a roadmap of high-value endeavors linked to business objectives that produce valuable outcomes in a series of small successes.

Many of us remember the 1997 book entitled *The Multidimensional Manager* (Richard Connelly, Robin McNeill, and Roland Mosimann, Cognos, Inc., 1997). It examined the partnership between decision-makers in companies worldwide and the people who provide them with better information using BI to drive better decisions. One of its key insights was that, as the complexity of businesses has grown, the majority of successful decision-makers concentrate their focus on a relatively small number of *sweet spots* of information that flow through the corporation.[7]

If we take the advice of the authors in *The Performance Manager,*[8] we can take this concept and follow those sweet spots in our effort to create a solid business alignment strategy. In other words, we can use the information trail to drill into the organization and investigate its core decision-making areas, which are typically these:

- Finance
- Marketing
- Sales
- Customer Service
- Product Development
- Operations
- Human Resources
- Information Technology

We know that we will, of necessity, be required to analyze the data, systems, reports, processes, and functions of these areas. Based on this information, we will be required to develop metrics and analytics, rate the effectiveness of the information to drive execution of the business strategy, and evolve our metrics to become more effective drivers of strategy execution. But who should be involved in this process?

This overall process will be much larger than any single individual because it impacts every area of the organization. This is not merely an IT project, nor simply a BI project. And it is not just a business unit project. It touches every key decision area in the organization. So identifying the stakeholders is a key element of success. These are the people in the organization who have an interest in ensuring that strategy moves smoothly to execution. And each of these people will have a role to play.

In other words, we need to assemble a team of key representatives from the following areas:

> "I've seen several projects fail because sufficient resources were not allocated to the initiative," says **John Boyer**, BI Enablement Lead at **Nielsen**. "Instead of appropriately allocating resources, focusing priorities, and involving the right stakeholders, they try to carve out time from individuals in silos who are already too busy."

- **Executive Involvement**—The executive team representatives who will champion the initiative, help define the business alignment strategy through prioritization, and create the performance management culture

- **Business Involvement**—The line-of-business representatives or subject matter experts who will define the business processes and metrics that are to be tied to corporate strategy and support and champion the management and execution

- **BI Team Involvement**—The BI team representatives who will innovate and define how different business metrics can be applied with data, systems, and processes and help to create successful execution within a BI environment

- **IT Team Involvement**—The various IT representatives who will ensure that all technologies are integrated and interconnected. They will apply technology to enable the business strategy—from information integration to database administration, security, and infrastructure

These representatives will act as the key leaders for the various areas within the organization that hold a stake in the outcome of the business alignment strategy. They must also be key players in helping to establish *credibility* for the overall team within their individual areas. It's a two-way street: they bring the knowledge of their decision-making culture from within their areas, but they must also communicate back—and champion— the vision of the business alignment strategy as it is formulated by the team. And working in partnership together, they can define the roadmap of initiatives that can be executed effectively through people, process, and technology to produce business impact.

Mapping Corporate Objectives to Bottom-Up Needs: Top-Down vs. Bottom-Up

All of us have experienced the difficulty of mapping the diverse operational needs of the company's managers and departments to the requirements and strategic goals of the larger organization. For many organizations, the conflicts between top-down (strategic) and bottom-up (tactical) approaches have sometimes become battlegrounds between business groups. And this difficulty manifests itself in the business alignment strategy: how do you prioritize these initiatives when an abundance of bottom-up tactical approaches exist in addition to the top-down strategy? Should we focus on individual business problems and roll solutions upward to a corporate-wide strategy? Or should we direct the strategy from the top, where the executive goals for the entire organization are more clearly understood? Understanding the pros and cons of both modalities will help us craft the best business alignment strategy for the organization.

The Bottom-Up Approach

When an individual decision area identifies a business problem, the first response is to implement a business solution that helps to solve the immediate goals of that entity. The solution may touch multiple departments or reach across to other decision areas. An example of this might be to provide a reporting or analytical tool that is easy to implement or to apply a legacy solution that has been customized to meet the specific needs of the decision-making area.

Many organizations may also approach business intelligence from a sequential technology perspective. A reporting system may be implemented on a silo of data, and one by one, the IT team may add additional data repositories from various business areas. Over time, there is the accomplishment of having a reporting system on a number of data sets, but it lacks a solid business alignment strategy that understands the outcomes and that links to top business objectives on what it is being used for. The initial reason, pain, or business need was not articulated, and when members of a business unit use the system, some of the information they need is not available or the information cannot be trusted. Little value might be recognized from the initiative.

There are pros and cons in approaching your business alignment strategy in this manner.

- **Bottom-Up Approach Pros**
    - » Individual departments can begin working together toward a tactical common goal that is easily understood by all involved.
    - » Solution implementation takes less time and expense in the short run.
    - » The solution can create a domino effect within the organization, leading other departments to implement similar solutions and/or scorecards.

- **Bottom-Up Approach Cons**
    - » The solution may not be directly tied to any larger organizational strategy.
    - » The solution's metrics—if they exist—may not be part of an organizational framework that informs the overall business strategy.
    - » As the solutions propagate within the organization, the various decision-areas can wander in their alignment to the organization's larger business strategy.

> "A bottom-up approach might be compared to building a house one room at a time without an overall design or even an idea of how big it needs to be," says **Kay Van De Vanter**, Enterprise BI Architect at **Boeing**. "In the end, you have a house, you may have spent lots of time and money, but it may not fit the needs of the family, and if standards and guidelines were not followed, the quality may be too poor to be able to use it as a home."

Most organizations are replete with bottom-up solution approaches, especially in those organizations that have grown through acquisition, rapid expansion, or long technology transitions.

The Top-Down Approach

By comparison, a top-down approach to implementing strategy first identifies the goals of the entire organization and then communicates how those goals will be measured across the enterprise. It defines the goals and the metrics, but it doesn't always define in detail the methods by which the various decision areas will achieve them.

There are, of course, pros and cons in approaching a strategic BI initiative in this manner.

- **Top-Down Approach Pros**
  - » The strategic objectives of the entire organization are cascaded downward and across the entire enterprise.
  - » Everybody acknowledges and understands what is expected.
  - » The strategy of the organization becomes linked directly to the operations of the organization.
  - » The executive decision-makers can support and fund the projects. They then drive the solutions throughout the organization to achieve the goals.
  - » Progress toward goals is measurable using a common syntax and agreed-upon metrics.

- **Top-Down Approach Cons**
  - » Implementation cycles can become lengthy as individual operational conflicts are reconciled.
  - » Top-down strategies require a significant cultural shift within the organization in which the overall executive goals supplant the immediate tactical preoccupations of individual decision-making entities.
  - » The long time-to-value process can derail a project when new priorities arise.

How Successful Companies Make It Work

Clearly, both approaches to implementing business intelligence initiatives are practiced by large and successful companies. It is rarely a lack of business strategy and execution methods that results in less-than-successful initiatives; most often, it's too many disparate strategies and initiatives operating in a disconnected and unprioritized business approach that result in a long time-to-value process or produce less-successful results. Melding a top-down with a bottom-up approach into something that functions within the organization is what the business alignment strategy is about.

Ultimately, this hybrid approach that is common in many growing organizations today is a transitional tactic that can be centrally managed through a strategic framework and organizational body. This approach can allow for managers to help define their own metrics, but it aligns priority and consistency in an organization via a business alignment strategy. Through an assessment of the current initiatives that are taking place through a bottom-up approach and an assessment of key priorities that are not currently covered, teams can better engage, decide on priorities, and align on key initiatives for new development. Whether it is managed by individuals in a business alignment function in the BI department, a separate steering committee, or individuals who closely align with a corporate strategy management function, it can help create higher value and impact in an organization.

Key Concept

This function or partnership will help coordinate cascading corporate strategy and prioritize and align business needs with the BI initiatives. It can prioritize key business initiatives, map them to existing bottom-up initiatives, and identify gaps, thereby defining the roadmap for delivering the series of successes that the organization needs in order to become more strategic in execution. It can also enable individuals with expertise in the business goals to partner with individuals who know what data is available. Then, the priority areas are implemented in a series of small successes in a rapid fashion. Providing an agile BI delivery via a series of smaller successes is key to maintaining momentum on the project and demonstrating value to the organization.

The tactic of implementing the business alignment approach—where top-down meets bottom up—across a consistent framework and communication system permits the following to occur within the organization:

- The decision area gets the implementation that it needs more quickly with less reiterations, due to strong alignment and expertise.

- The solution provides "cultural capital" within the organization as a series of "wins" for the BI process.

- The BI process can be extended to the next project in another decision area.

But why should this hybrid strategy be centrally managed?

By bringing the diverse BI processes into a focused framework, the company can ultimately be guided to a comprehensive, consistent strategic planning mechanism. It will achieve this transition by working with the same Key Performance Indicators (KPIs), sourced from a common information resource.

Developing Metrics and the KPI Design

Obviously, defining standard metrics and turning them into something measurable is not an easy task. This complete effort requires a strong partnership between executives, strategy managers, IT, BI professionals or business analysts, and the business unit managers. The business unit managers define what they are seeking to measure, and the IT and BI teams help to connect the metrics to the reality of the data.

The Performance Manager: A Framework for Strategy

The previously mentioned book, *The Performance Manager*, provides a framework that enables the combined team of BI professionals and business unit managers to guide the conversation to the sweet spots of information.

Within the framework described in *The Performance Manager*, each decision area (Finance, Marketing, Sales, and so on) is guided by core content of each corresponding set of information sweet spots. Using this framework, each area can organize the sweet spots into matrixes of measurements: a) goals, b) metrics, and c) a hierarchical set of dimensions.

In every discipline, specific sweet spots of information that are common across most organizations will create valuable results linked to common top business priorities.

It is a common challenge that when BI teams engage with the various business units, their partners do not know what metrics to measure or what information is available to them. The Performance Manager methodology can form the beginning of the framework from which we can start to explore the information sweet spots that drive the decision-making processes. It's a simple model upon which we can build the architecture of our business strategy, with each decision area and function standing on its own. Figure 1.1 depicts an example.

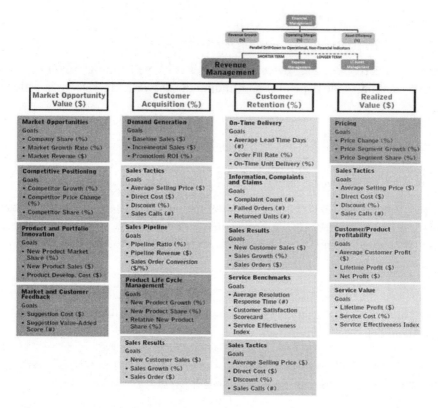

Figure 1.1: A cross-functional perspective on decision areas.[9]

But this model is more than a list of particularly important information sweet spots. The framework charts how individual decision areas and functions are in fact slices of a broader, integrated framework for performance management across the entire company.

While the authors of *The Performance Manager* acknowledge that "Overly grand, top-down enterprise designs tend to fail, or don't live up to their full promise, due to the major technical and cultural challenges involved," this model is designed for precisely such an incremental approach. Decision areas empower individual performance managers to achieve immediate goals in their areas of responsibility. As we combine these goals across decision areas, we can create a scorecard for that function. Then, as we realize performance success, we can build upon it to solve the greater challenge posed by cross-functional collaboration around shared strategies and goals.

Constructing a Methodology Toward Performance Management

The importance of *The Performance Manager* is its methodology. Every decision-making cycle depends upon finding the answer to three core questions (Figure 1.2):

- How are we doing?
- Why?
- What should we be doing?

As a framework for creating a model of the business, this methodology provides a means of measuring our progress. It also enables us to create scorecards and dashboards that monitor the business with metrics to find answers to *How are we doing?*

Likewise, the model uses reporting and analysis to provide the capacity to look at historical data, analyze underlying trends, and identify anomalies to understand the *Why?*

And finally, the framework enables us to plan, predict, and forecast to depict a reliable perspective on the future to answer *What should we be doing?*

But the key insight—one that we fully embrace—is the prerequisite of integrating all of these capabilities across *all* the decision-making areas to enable us to respond to changes happening in our businesses.

To ensure consistency in answering these fundamental performance questions, you must integrate functionality not just within each one, but across them all. Knowing what happened without finding out why is of little use. Knowing why something happened but being unable to plan and make the necessary changes is also of limited value.

Figure 1.2: Informed, aligned decisions and actions.[10]

Moreover, a key insight that we've discovered is how the strategy must function: it must be *seamless* across the full network of performance managers.

For instance, just as the core questions are connected, the answers must be based upon a common understanding of metrics, data dimensions, and data definitions shared by all the decision-makers in the organization.

Determining Priorities

Determining the priority of decision areas, or sweet spots, to conquer in your business alignment strategy is relatively straightforward: each business process is assessed for its business value in terms of the revenue obtained or the expense it controls—two of the highest-value areas for managing performance. It is also assessed against top annual objectives. A simple scale can be applied to each business demand to rate the overall value to the organization, differentiating low-value business issues and very high-value business issues.

Figure 1.3 provides a sample template for rating these priorities for an organization. This rating can also contain an inventory of the availability of this information and the successes that already exist. This requires a detailed analysis of available IT assets and an understanding of how those assets are being used.

By analyzing the key elements of each business issue, an associated KPI can be created, detailing the importance of the information created by individual sources.

Prioritization Roadmap Matrix

Corporate Alignment	Business Issue	Ratings				
Stakeholder & Business Area	Request	Corporate Priority	Revenue Impact	Expense Reduction	Information Gap	Quick Win
John Doe, Sales	Pipeline Analysis	1	1	3	1	N
	Customer Analysis	2	1	1	3	N
Jane Smith, Operations	Delivery Analysis	2	2	3	2	N
	Claims	3	2	1	3	N
John Smith, Marketing	Demand Generation	3	1	3	2	Y
	1 High Priority					
	2 Medium Priority					
	3 Low Priority					

Figure 1.3: A rating of business issues for a sample organization.

Analysis and Priority

Once basic priorities and ratings are identified, they can be categorized in a business alignment strategy that defines a roadmap for success. The roadmap provides a timeline prioritizing "must do now" vs. "invest for the future" vs. "de-prioritize." Factors influencing this prioritization include:

- **Key Corporate Priority**—Relation to the top goals of the enterprise

- **High Revenue Impact**—The assets that have the closest link to the revenue goals

- **Significant Expense Reduction**—The assets that provide the best opportunities to improve efficiency and achieve direct cost savings

- **High Information Gap**—The assets in which poor information inhibits decision-making

- **Quick-Win Opportunities**—Correlations between already-available assets where there are opportunities for a quick win

Rolling these assets upward toward the business goals—along with the metrics associated with their values—can permit us to look across both the demand and the supply side of the information and identify those opportunities that will create a series of small successes—something that, as mentioned previously, is critical to maintaining momentum and demonstrating value over time.

Defining the Business Case

With a roadmap that both defines a business alignment strategy for a BI or performance management initiative and links to top corporate objectives and business outcomes, the business case and value impact of the initiative becomes easier to articulate. To define the business case, we can use the business value hierarchy that was mentioned in the introduction. This business value hierarchy provides us with the understanding that investments in BI can generate three basic sources of value:

- An increase in IT efficiency
- A gain in business efficiency
- Improved business effectiveness

According to a recent *Computerworld* study,[11] 67 percent of organizations cited a lack of time, budget, or resources as inhibitors to a successful BI initiative. Such issues are often the result of an inability to demonstrate the concrete cross-organizational value of an initiative. Focusing on these three sets of value provides a strong and compelling business case. And while this may seem simplistic, the business case for many organizations is too often a difficult task because the alignment between the various stakeholders—business units, central IT and BI teams, and the executive management team—is not strong enough to articulate a compelling justification or clear outcome of the initiative. Often, IT efficiencies such as total cost of ownership (TCO) or expense controls are the only justification. In many cases, business efficiencies can be articulated—such as time savings or resource efficiencies—but these indirect benefits are difficult to quantify.

The true value and the core of a business case is strengthened through the outcomes that will be achieved from the overall business alignment strategy for the BI initiative. With outcomes as the core, a comprehensive strategy can be understood to allow an organization to make better decisions faster and thus use time more effectively, focusing more attention on issues that matter—the *sweet spots* that most accurately depict the company's performance. A justification at this level will produce better understanding, alignment, and a focus on common objectives.

As a proven practice, organizations that are successful at BI initiatives will articulate the three sets of value in their business case in order to produce successful results and understanding. Let's take a deeper look at examples of each of these values that should be applied to the business case.

Proven
Practice

Increasing IT Efficiency

Obviously, improving IT efficiency is an important source of value, with expense savings at its core through reduction of license costs, resources, and associated hardware costs.

A total cost of ownership discussion will become a strong part of the business case, given that most consideration is typically given to the visible license cost of the software, not to the total costs of a solution—the costs of training, evaluation, consulting, hardware, support, and other areas that need to be considered. If you multiply the costs across all these areas for multiple toolsets and consider the savings that can be achieved by limiting the number of tools, you can deliver a fairly compelling expense-driven discussion.

However, if the BI business strategy project is championed and managed only by the IT department, executive management's backing may not be as strong. Why? Because the project may be perceived as seeking only to refine existing processes rather than to discover new opportunities, which can result in a continual cycle of cutting costs and resources to improve efficiency and the bottom line. So, as important as increasing IT efficiency is for organizations, it creates a less compelling case to focus *solely* on this issue while making a business case.

IT Efficiency Examples

Direct total cost of ownership (TCO) savings in use of IT resources:

- Cost savings or cost avoidance such as through software or hardware license savings and use

- Services, consulting, training efficiencies

- Faster IT response time, improved allocation of work and productivity, employee labor

- Reuse of technical assets and proven methodologies

Increasing Business Efficiency

A stronger business case can be made for the BI investment if we focus on business efficiency. Increased productivity of business users, automation of manual processes that result in shorter sales cycles, faster finance processes, or the ability to reduce inefficiencies and duplication can generate a compelling justification for a project.

Business Efficiency Examples

Productivity savings in terms of business users' time to perform both transactions and decision-making:

- Faster close cycles and improved times to complete work or projects, resulting in cost savings

- Better resource allocation and increased productivity

- Cost savings of time through automation of processes

Improving Business Effectiveness

The third source of value is business effectiveness. This is the outcome of measuring, monitoring, understanding, and planning against an objective and achieving the intended results. Ultimately, the definitive reason for developing a comprehensive BI business strategy is to improve business performance. But how can we measure that improvement?

Most often, the improvements will demonstrate the ability to meet top corporate objectives, or revenue or expense goals, that were prioritized in the alignment strategy. Almost all of these benefits will take the form of higher revenues, lower costs and expenses, reduced risk, or some combination of these three.

Business Effectiveness Examples

Improved business performance from faster and more informed decision-making:

- Higher customer value
- Improved product mix (margins)
- Better sales pipeline conversion ratio
- Enhanced customer retention
- Greater production yields
- Better order fulfillment
- Faster collections
- Lower production costs
- Reduced risk/reduced impact of risks

Summary

As we pointed out at the beginning of this chapter, only one in five companies is able to successfully execute on its business strategy. So how do you become one of those organizations that achieve success? We believe that using a business alignment strategy for effectively prioritizing and linking the corporate strategy—from a top-down approach to the bottom-up tactics—with BI as a way to measure, monitor, plan, and execute on corporate strategy can help organizations better achieve successful outcomes. It is the first step of the journey to business intelligence excellence, and it's a repeatable way to move your organization into a better position to achieve the business goals of the enterprise.

"Providing business value goes beyond simply reducing cost," says **Brian Green**, Manager of Business Intelligence and Performance Management at **BlueCross BlueShield of Tennessee**. "For example, we were able to deploy a financial performance management application much faster than originally estimated due to the prior investments we had already made in developing a financial data mart and our integrated business intelligence deployment strategy. By leveraging existing technology investments, skills, and resources, there were a number of efficiencies that were created, which resulted in a faster time to implement our solution. We are now working on an initiative to further increase value by enabling shorter financial forecasting cycles."

Checklist of Recommended Approaches

☑ Leverage success in your organization. Assess the current situation in your organization to better determine the high-value and low-value initiatives that already exist.

☑ Prioritize decision areas, or sweet spots of information, by mapping key areas of value against corporate objectives, revenue opportunities, and expense savings. This is critical to producing high-value results. Prepare a value matrix that demonstrates the areas of highest value and importance.

☑ Create a roadmap of priorities that results in a series of high-value wins to kick the project off to a successful start. Prepare the roadmap and timeline based on the prioritized sweet spots, and map to existing projects that exist today in your organization.

☑ Align and produce strategy in partnership with various stakeholders to gain momentum. Create a map of stakeholders that corresponds to the sweet spots of information to collaborate in determining priorities. Ensure that a business alignment team—whether fixed or virtual—is created to deliver consistency and priority across business alignment strategy. Determine who from your organization needs to be involved in this team.

☑ Prepare the business case. Ensure it contains IT efficiency, business efficiency, and business effectiveness outcomes to demonstrate maximum value.

Business Alignment Strategy Overview

Overview

Describe the initiative at a high level.

Corporate Objectives

Describe your top corporate objectives and identify how they impact the strategy.

Assessment

Determine successful initiatives that exist today that can be leveraged.

Roadmap

Describe the top decision areas—or sweet spots—that will be tackled in order of priority, and rate them to determine the timeline and roadmap.

Value Outcomes

Describe the IT efficiency, business efficiency, and business effectiveness outcomes.

Business Case

Demonstrate the costs, resources, and expenses valued against the value impact they will enable.

Stakeholders

Describe the project team and stakeholders (assess your champions and your roadblocks).

Chapter 2

Organizational and Behavioral Strategy

On the surface, it's easy to see why every organization should already be implementing a Business Intelligence (BI) strategy. However, wanting this capability and actually making it happen are two very different things. According to Cindi Howson's "Successful BI Survey," user adoption remains low at only 24 percent, and many factors that influence a project's success are organizational and behavioral rather than technical in nature.[1] For BI initiatives to become strategic, they require input and interaction that is much broader in scope than the average IT project, and they demand early buy-in and collaboration between multiple business and IT entities across the organization. The need for early buy-in is especially true of senior management, but it also requires in-depth support in each of the key decision-making areas identified in Chapter 1.

In many organizations, when it comes to a strategic BI initiative, politics and culture can easily derail a project. Navigating politics and culture is always a key challenge. What do we mean here? Challenges we've struggled with include gaining user adoption; managing change; getting acceptance, support, and consensus across executives, line-of-business managers, and IT; and promoting and enforcing technology standards through strong governance and oversight by the various management teams. Often, many issues of politics and culture can be overcome through inclusion and communication. Many politically charged situations occur because there is a lack of these critical components:

- Understanding of the plan by the stakeholders (both IT and business)

- Understanding of the value and what it means specifically to the stakeholders

- A change-management plan that will provide stakeholders with confidence and help them make a transition

- Alignment and a common language between business and IT

- Buy-in, promotion, and support by executive leadership

- Proof points and/or demonstrated support from other groups that have been successful

- An ability to determine ROI or to communicate the tangible and intangible values of BI that can usually be resolved via internal or external references

To obtain the necessary support, we believe you'll need to study and understand the unique business culture of your organization. Creating an organizational and behavioral strategy that achieves a strong foundation of communication—built to incrementally achieve some *wins*—and developing an ongoing campaign to maintain the momentum for your overall strategy can increase success.

The guidance in this chapter will help you to recognize and avoid derailment factors that are common to most organizations as they transition to a strategic initiative. We will examine the following:

- **Cultural Sensitivity**—Obstacles to look for as you assess your organization and come to understand the politics and culture that exist

- **Executive Support**—Understanding of how critical executive support is for a BI initiative and suggestions for how to engage the executive team in the project

- **Organizational Structures**—Understanding of the value of the organizational structure for a BI initiative, common design approaches, and funding models

- **User Adoption**—Factors that influence adoption, tactics that can be used, and considerations as to what may be hindering adoption

- **Communication and Training Strategies**—Approaches to communicating with your stakeholders, keeping knowledge levels high, and marketing and showcasing techniques that have been used to maintain momentum

Understanding Your Business Culture

Our experience has shown that politics and culture are intense operational factors within our organizations as they relate to the BI initiative. The dynamics are always unique within each company, are often personal, are many times difficult to navigate, and usually are institutionally complex to influence. The larger the organization or the longer it has been in operation, the harder it can seem to influence substantial change. Yet all of us have seen our business cultures change and flourish, and BI has helped to facilitate that change.

> "Technology is the easy part. Computers are predictable," says **John Boyer.** "It's the people that are the challenge. Don't underestimate the effect of change on the human element."

But there's a catch: change will often take time, and successful change occurs in step-by-step increments. It requires partnerships and measurements of individual successes.

Why is it so hard? After all, isn't corporate productivity what it's all about? What are the obstacles? Many are simply cultural artifacts from the organization's history of growth. But often there is resistance from within individual cadres of the business organization itself.

Politics and culture enter the picture in many forms. Often, employees won't want to use the tools they are provided. They find that changing their habits—those age-old, familiar ways of doing things—is challenging, and the value may not be understood. It must be demonstrated that it is not just a new "tool" but a strategic investment in themselves and alignment with business and/or IT strategy. It's possible they need the proper training to accomplish new requirements or need additional support from the Business Intelligence department or Center of Competency—the organizational structure put in place to make the endeavor successful. Sometimes, they worry about accountability and believe that a change in the familiar processes of their jobs will uncover something they would rather not reveal. Often, they don't understand how the new processes that will be implemented can benefit the overall organization, or they fear that the change may dilute the value that they are already providing to the organization. They do not see the common objective that is being sought. Or, finally, they resist because they feel they were not consulted in the process—perhaps because they had needs that were different from those of the rest of the organization.

While these are all natural fears, we've found they can become real obstacles to the success of your BI initiative, obstacles that need to be acknowledged as part of the dominant corporate culture. Each individual and functional area has to understand how the change will benefit their own team, and ultimately, they need to understand how it benefits the organization.

Communicating the Goals

While people and processes may seem to be the biggest challenge to a successful BI initiative—especially in organizations where past information processes have become rigid or siloed—they can be changed. And the first step is to communicate, clarifying the stated strategic goals of the organization and the value that can be provided. This often means ensuring you are using the language that makes sense to each individual user in his or her functional area, communicating the business alignment strategy that was formed in Chapter 1, and explaining how the new process will help to achieve those goals. The values and outcomes as they relate to each individual area are the key drivers for alignment.

In some cases, how an individual's isolated job intersects with the larger goals of the organization is unclear. We've found that when someone is running independently against the strategy, it's often simply because they haven't connected the dots from corporate strategy to their individual area of expertise.

> "Reluctance to engage in a strategic endeavor can stem from a lack of understanding and alignment," says **Bill Frank**, Manager, BI Practice, **Johnson & Johnson**. "Having an inclusive approach and a strong communication strategy is the best way to ensure needs are being met for the successful outcome of the organization."

Without clear communication of the direction, the value of and goals for managing performance, and the requirements for those changes, the task of implementing change through BI can quickly become derailed. This communication is necessary not in just one department or decision area, but across the entire organization. This message for those changes has to be clear and concise. It has to connect each individual to the value that is important to them—and to the benefit of the organization.

What does this change look like?

Transitioning the Culture by Active Team-Based Collaboration

We've found that one important behavioral change that fosters good results is rewarding successful participants rather than imposing penalties on those who don't engage in the strategy. In other words, we need to motivate individual departments and decision areas and transition them from *passive information resources* into *enthusiastic stakeholders* in the BI process itself.

How do you accomplish that?

> "People can be obstructive, perhaps not intentionally," says **John Boyer**. "Give them the benefit of the doubt; they are likely acting on the information they have. They may not have the whole picture. In our role, we can help them make that connection."

> "You need to make sure the key stakeholders understand and invest in the BI strategy," says **Kay Van De Vanter**. "Otherwise, you are constantly pushing against the mountain."

One of the most successful means is by creating internal business and IT team communities and structures that reassess the information processes within the key decision areas, comparing them against the information goals of the larger BI strategy. This includes a formalized structure that brings together the BI team members, IT professionals, business analysts, and the larger community of stakeholders who will work closely to achieve success. In our experience, this technique accomplishes a number of things:

- **Educates**—All of us have seen how creating a team can more fully educate the participants in the overall BI initiative, the alignment to strategy, and the value it provides while helping to identify how individual job functions contribute as elements within the structure of the BI process.

- **Supports Structure**—Many of us have witnessed how the creation of internal teams creates operational support for the decision-makers themselves. It facilitates the ability of decision-makers to communicate the business strategy down through the individual decision areas, while reinforcing the internal organizational structure within that area. In the process, we've seen how it often provides visible recognition to those on the team who contribute most effectively.

- **Reveals Obstacles**—Each of us have experienced how a vibrant team—working diligently to define and describe individual business problems—can operate as a mechanism to reveal real-world operational obstacles early. Often, these obstacles would otherwise have remained hidden until they were discovered during an implementation phase. Instead, uncovering them early, within the team structure and processes, enabled the team to reconcile the problems *before* they became critical.

- **Inspires Collaboration**—No man is an island, and no team exists in a vacuum. We've seen how various business teams working together—within a decision area that is communicating with the BI team—have permitted valuable cross-pollination of new ideas.

- **Creates Buy-in**—Teaming business unit stakeholders with BI professionals and IT experts creates the opportunity for buy-in by the team members who were initially reluctant. It also provides a valuable means of communicating success within the organization. Each team's success has the potential to become a self-reinforcing mechanism for the entire project, and many times that success is virally broadcast to other areas in the corporation.

"We are seeing an increase in organizations in the industry that are implementing both BI departments and virtual BI communities," says **Tracy Harris**, Senior Manager of BI Excellence at **IBM**. "These organizations are seeing higher success rates by having dedicated resources to manage the strategy and an open line of communication with the various cross-functional stakeholders. Together, they can work together to reach the strategic goals of the organization."

This collaborative approach changes the business culture and is, in our experience, highly effective. Of course, there are many ways to describe it, but we see this as *building the culture*. By aligning business strategy with identifiable metrics and then increasing performance through reengineering the information process, each decision area will start to witness an increase in capabilities and a profound streamlining of business efficiencies. These teams begin to see success building, which helps to develop their passion and engages them in the strategy.

By gaining a thorough understanding of both the existing culture within your organization and the community of stakeholders and partners that are needed to achieve success, you can begin to define the organizational and behavioral strategy that will need to be implemented to achieve higher success rates.

Executive Support[2]

The good news today is that most organizations have a strong level of support—and even push—from the executive suite to use BI and analytics to understand the business. However, it may be occurring in silos and may not necessarily be a strategic endeavor that is sponsored by a partnered executive team. So, when we speak of executive support, we are seeing that bringing a number of executives on board for a strategic endeavor is necessary; they work together on the strategy and the ways it can be deployed across the organization rather than in silos. And we believe that team building—partnering business personnel with BI personnel—is a critical tactic, but it's a tactic that works best if the ranks of the senior management itself are fully supportive of the initiative.

Executives can build alignment with the strategy by lending their support through the four *E*s: encourage, engage, evangelize, and enlist. Without executives on board to encourage, engage, and evangelize—and to enlist resources as they are needed—the typical BI and Performance Management initiative can take substantially longer or fail altogether. So, how did we accomplish it? We've seen the enlistment process vary quite a bit within each of our organizations.

We've found that the business leaders in the organization sometimes need to be sold on the idea of standardization; they need to understand the value of a collaborative Performance Management initiative or the value of broad user adoption. Other times, simply educating the key stakeholders about the goals of Performance Management will help to open the lines of communication between regions and departments and prevent a silo-driven approach to an implementation. All of us have faced this challenge at one time or another, and we've discovered that navigating the business culture of the executives and building their support is one of the most important factors leading to BI and PM success.

Mining for Executive Buy-In

We've seen that the acceptance of BI and PM within the business culture is heavily influenced from the top down, but as the message cascades through the ranks, it can become diluted or, due to the busy nature of an executive role, it can be forgotten if not kept top of mind. Building and maintaining momentum for BI is not only an important goal, it's *crucial* in order to transform key executives into actual champions for the value of BI.

How do you accomplish this?

It starts with recognizing the goal. What's needed in the organization is more than the cursory nod from senior management. It's active support. We need those executive champions to lead the troops toward the goals of BI and Performance Management.

They also need to recognize the real cultural obstacles and talk about the need for a cultural shift within the company's ranks.

Our individual experiences have taught us that successful enterprise-wide deployments *can and will* change the information culture of the corporation, but there is a catch: to get to that change, we also need to change *our own* relationships with the wider enterprise. We have to break through the walls that separate our decision area from the rest of the organization. We need to be willing to engage management, to be sensitive to their issues, and to speak their business language.

These are clearly not simple tasks. They require an awareness of the obstacles that lie in the road ahead and a willingness to address those obstacles constructively. In other words, we need to foster a new level of partnership between IT and other key decision-makers. They must become our ultimate stakeholders and our clients.

Understanding Senior Executive Priorities

Getting executives' attention to recognize the value of and understand BI and Performance Management can be difficult when they may be struggling with their own responsibilities. Nonetheless, they're probably looking for help in alleviating their problems, though they may not be looking at BI and Performance Management as solutions. Keep that in mind before initiating your approach.

The first task is to understand their pain points—what hurts and where—in *their* context and *their* language. So here are some tips.

Table 2.1 lists some key roles present in most organizations, but remember that each organization is different, and roles are often fungible within the corporation. So get to know your unique organization's key roles, and then hone your message appropriately.

Table 2.1: Key Executive Roles			
Role	**Responsibilities**	**Top Priorities**	**Requirements**
CEO	Setting strategic direction and articulating corporate vision	• Ensuring top business goals are met successfully, on time and on budget • Ensuring the vision and future strategy is set for the organization	• Convey the message to subordinates • Ensure that priorities are funded appropriately
CIO	Innovating to improve the business	• Enabling business innovation • Improving customer satisfaction • Reducing business costs • Creating competitive advantage	• Understand the issues in business terms while understanding the IT benefit and value • Avoid viewing challenge and opportunity exclusively from a technology perspective
CFO	Managing regulatory and financial processes	• Measuring and monitoring business performance • Meeting fiduciary and statutory requirements • Monitoring process and business improvement	• Understand strategic and productivity benefits, global process ownership, and integration • Turn data into usable information • Turn usable information into meaningful insights • Establish a data governance framework
Line-of-Business Executive	Driving day-to-day operational performance	• Improving profit • Increasing productivity • Reducing business risk	• Connect with business-area subject matter experts • Find champions willing to collaborate on identifying solutions • Solicit broad-based support • Drive adoption elsewhere across the business

While it may seem fairly obvious to say that we've found that it's not effective to try enlisting executives within one decision area by speaking only of the value of another area of the company, this is how the initiative is communicated in many organizations. As an example, an IT team may speak of how the consolidated strategy will improve service-level agreement (SLA) times, decrease total costs, or increase IT efficiencies. Or a finance team may demonstrate how it will improve financial processes and cut expenses. In fact, in attempting to gain buy-in, it's important to avoid the temptation of approaching all senior executives with the same strategy, as they may not see how their area will benefit in the sample outcomes that are shared. You need to adapt your messages depending on who you're aiming to enlist. So understanding each executive's unique responsibilities is crucial, and communicating in their language, identifying the benefits that will be of value to them, is the key. This point may seem obvious, but you'd be surprised by how often an opportunity to gain support is wasted because the wrong executive is pitched the wrong message.

Key Concept

Tactics for Engaging the Executive Set

We've found there are many different kinds of tactics for engaging management and executives, but we've narrowed down the list to a few key recommendations:

- **Speak the Language of Business**—You must demonstrate the value of the BI and Performance Management initiative in business-focused, non-technical terms.

- **Know Your Leaders' Key Pain Points**—Every part of every organization feels some sort of pain. The key to maximizing the buy-in potential lies in under- standing those *unique* pains before approaching leadership. What are they? How do they affect operations and planning? How are they being prioritized? How can the BI and PM initiative help?

- **Focus on Messaging**—Senior leaders love to know what's going on and always seek to be on the winning team. Internally communicate key wins to them and their stakeholders to maximize buy-in potential. Articulate the value proposition of these wins—for example, a business unit increased sales, improved marketing campaign effectiveness, or closed the books in hours instead of days—and use business-friendly terms in the process.

- **Don't Ask for Money**—Never expect leaders to sign a blank check. Dollars are the last thing to mention when initiating contact with a senior leader. Frame the discussion in terms of value to the organization, business justification, and long-term benefits to competitiveness. And when you do communicate the cost, you need to communicate the quantifiable and indirect value they will be receiving as a counter.

- **Start Small**—Don't expect senior leaders to instantly understand the BI and PM value proposition. Be prepared to suggest smaller-scale pilot projects to prove the concept with a series of quick, high-profile wins to demonstrate the value and gain executive trust. Follow up with a roadmap to migrate the organization from siloed analytics to a corporate BI strategy.

- **Respect Their Time**—Have your elevator speech ready and well-organized.

Keep the Conversation Going

We've found that just because a senior leader buys into BI and Performance Management doesn't mean he or she will be on board forever. Far from it. If anything, buy-in isn't so much achieved as it is maintained. Plan on continuing to evolve the relationship with executive-level stakeholders to ensure their support remains strong over time.

A BI strategy demands a certain degree of marketing savvy. Even if you've always been in IT, you'll need to learn how to *sell*. You have to play a sales role to maintain ongoing support at this level. Be prepared to regularly approach your executives and show them, in concrete terms, how you're going to cut costs, generate more revenue, or otherwise improve the way things work. There's a very strong internal sales aspect to maintaining executive buy-in over time.

> "Gaining buy-in is ongoing," says **Brian Green**. "It's definitely not something you achieve and then put on the back burner. You have to constantly keep the value-add focused on your key business objectives if you're going to keep their buy-in."

Use statistics and analyst research that may help to sway your executives to support the cause. As an example, Nucleus Research, Inc., conducted a study[3] in which they found that Business Intelligence and Performance Management performed the following functions:

- **Improved Productivity by up to 20 Percent**—Implementing a comprehensive BI/PM strategy can increase the productivity of workers involved in reporting, finance, or analysis by up to 20 percent.

- **Cut Staffing Costs by up to 15 Percent**—Efficiencies created by BI/PM have enabled line-of-business organizations to reduce reporting and analysis staff by up to 15 percent.

- **Reduced Assets by up to 15 Percent**—Inventory amounts, accounts receivable, and other assets that are purchased and maintained on the balance sheet were cut by up to 15 percent after BI/PM systems were successfully implemented.

Of course, every organization will find its own area's savings. But the two key messages we've found that resonate with our senior executives are a) "Doing better" requires both "working smarter" and efficiency across all decision areas; and b) achieving that smarter behavioral and cultural environment requires maximizing the use of BI and embracing Performance Management.

Value of an Organizational Structure

Where do you start in building the organizational team that can empower BI and PM? How can a team be implemented? To whom does it report? Is it a part of IT, or is it a part of the business organization within the corporation? What value will such a team bring to the organization? These are questions that need to be seriously considered before the organization embarks on any enterprise-wide BI strategy.

Let's speak from experience and from the perspective of the organization's bottom line.

Many of our organizations are responding to the need for strategic BI and PM by creating working teams of IT and BI, both virtual (such as a "community of interest" and structured (such as a BI department). These teams are often called the BI Competency Center (BICC).

In a recent study by the Business Applications Research Center, it was discovered that "Companies with BICCs outperformed those without competency centers in every issue."[4] The study found that user satisfaction levels improved;

greater penetration of the tools existed within the organization; and notable improvements in alignment with strategy, process, and data improvements were achieved.

We have seen that the institutionalization of a BI structure can also help organizations lower their total cost of ownership (TCO). BICCs help to drive a lower TCO of our Business Intelligence and technology solutions with reduced implementation costs and eased deployment risk. They accomplish this through the following:

- **The Consolidation of Information, Skills, and Knowledge**—BICCs deliver higher and faster rates of adoption of the complete BI lifecycle. Moreover, they provide a "single version of the truth" across the entire enterprise, which can improve user satisfaction and self-service. By bringing expertise together, repeatable practices are formed, driving faster time to market, shared knowledge, and increased productivity.

- **The Creation and Institutionalization of Proven Practices and Standards**—BICCs adopt and share proven practices and enforce BI standards through registration and guidance and have the ability to identify new opportunities to leverage BI. The impact of standards and shared practices results in a more efficient alignment of the technologies to strategic goals (competitive differentiation/regulatory requirements) and clarifies the vision for future coordinated BI. This improves costs from a software license, services, training, hardware, and support perspective and improves time efficiency and the ability to leverage skills.

We've also used BICCs to educate our key stakeholders about the advantages of employing BI and Performance Management. In fact, our BICCs help to open and build the lines of communication between regions and departments to prevent a silo-driven approach to implementation. In doing so, we can engineer each BI solution so that it will clearly demonstrate its value through the breadth, depth, completeness, accuracy, and timeliness of information available throughout the enterprise.

Defining the BI Competency Center (BICC)[5]

The BICC organizational structure groups people with interrelated disciplines, domains of knowledge, experiences, and skills for the purpose of promoting expertise throughout an organization. Sometimes, this team is known by other names:

- BI Department
- BI Center of Practice
- BI Community
- BI Center of Excellence (BICoE)
- BI Center of Knowledge
- BI Community of Practice
- BI Technology Services
- Data Mining and Information Delivery

For the purpose of this document, we will label it a BICC for simplicity. But, by whatever moniker, the general purposes of this team include these:

- Promoting and delivering business value through a *consistent set* of BI skills, standards, and practices.

- Enabling successful BI deployments through the development of people, technologies, and processes. The methodology used is designed to make successes *repeatable* in ways that reflect the needs of the entire organization or division.

- Creating measurements of success that are relevant to the entire organization, not just a single team, department, or project.

In most organizations, the BICC is a formal, organized department. We see this as increasingly important as the market dynamics and speed of decision-making pressure organizations to be highly transparent, proficient, and effective in their daily operating and decision-making.

Today, we see an increasing need for IT and BI to address business challenges:

- **Do More with Less**—Reduce our capital expenditures and operational expenses.

- **Reduce Risk**—Ensure the right levels of security and resiliency across all of our business data and processes.

- **Provide Higher-Quality Services**—Improve our quality of services and deliver new services that help the business grow and reduce cost.

- **Open New Opportunities**—Increase our ability to quickly deliver new services to capitalize on opportunities while containing costs and managing risk.

- **Create Efficiencies**—Create repeatable processes and leverage solutions, infrastructure, and resources.

- **Increase Alignment**—Align business goals and monitor them in order to execute successfully.

A BICC significantly assists in these tasks. But let's explore these tasks in a little more detail.

We have seen that if BI is to extend beyond mere *tactical* deployments to become a broader-based *strategic* solution, it requires a more managed, predictable approach. A BICC can define the knowledge, standards, and resources needed to make this happen. A BICC is essential to the strategic deployment of BI because it achieves these goals:

- Maximizes the efficiency, use, and quality of your BI across all lines of business through standards and reusability

- Leads to BI deployments that have higher success and deliver more value, at less cost, in less time

- Drives end-user adoption to ensure its success (simply providing BI to an increasing number of information consumers doesn't guarantee more people will use it)

- Helps close the gap between what the business needs and what IT delivers

- Enables business agility and improved technology management, helping to drive overall business efficiency

In our experience, a BICC enables repeatable, successful BI deployments through the development of people, technologies, and processes. Moreover, it accomplishes this in ways that make sense to the entire organization or division, rather than just a single project.

Organizational Design Approaches

So how did our organizations set up our BICCs? What are some of the lessons we've learned? While each of our experiences is different and aligned to our own organizational and cultural factors, there is a set of common elements. And we've found that the most successful BICCs are formed through a pragmatic development effort that *matures* over time. We recommend these tactics:

- Start small.

- Think strategically.

- Systematically accelerate.

Key Concept

What we have discovered is that there is no "one size fits all" approach. Every organization has a unique culture and organizational approach, and the BICC must fit within it. Establishing a successful BICC depends on the right planning. Organizations that take a measured, well-managed approach that stresses synergy between people, processes, and technologies are more likely to succeed. The success of this approach is that it will gain wider support and contribute to significant cost savings while it takes business intelligence to the next strategic level.

BICC models vary according to the needs of the organization. Figure 2.1 depicts several different organizational possibilities for BICCs.

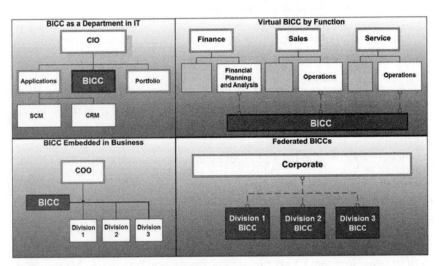

Figure 2.1: Different organizational models for BICCs.[6]

An individual BICC may initially start as an IT-only initiative, designed to focus on consolidating the system knowledge necessary to ensure a consistent enterprise strategy for BI. Or the model may be one that is based upon line-of-business requirements, focusing on functional business skills and specific capabilities sponsored by business executives. Some BICCs are centralized at a corporate-office level, while others are loose networks or regional and divisional federated teams made up of business and IT personnel.

However, all organizational structures tend to change, adjust, and mature over time. Many times, BICCs evolve in synch with the developmental life cycle of your BI tools and their level of implementation. For example, competencies and focus within the BICC will differ in early stages of ideation, planning, development, and maintenance. Early competencies may need to focus on adoption and evangelization, whereas, in later stages, the BICC may need to demonstrate a stronger role in articulating proven practices.

No matter where the BICC resides, a key element is that it brings together several functions in an organization for alignment and is the coordinating body for a larger community of stakeholders.

Goals and Objectives of the BICC

In our experience, the BICC—whether centralized, de-centralized, based on full-time employees or a virtual set of community skills—searches for the right technologies for the most complete, relevant, and consistent view of information. It attempts to implement and/or support the implementation of the best metrics to help drive the corporate strategy of growth and profitability. It tries to use the most effective organizational design and business model to help the company achieve a shared view of how the company operates by leveraging information to the fullest potential. The common functions of a BICC can therefore vary.

Of course, it's important again to note that no one-size BICC fits all. The BICC scope should be based on your organizational needs and the dynamic considerations of human capital, managed process, culture, and infrastructure (hardware and software). The graphic in Figure 2.2 illustrates some of the elements to address when building a solid foundation for your BICC.

Key
Concept

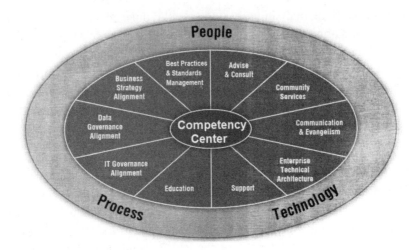

Figure 2.2: BICC functions within the organization.[7]

- **Best Practices and Standards Management**—Provide a clear process and repository for approving and sharing best practices and standards for the enterprise.

- **Advise and Consult**—Provide a functional area of business with advice, guidance, mentoring, and "internal consulting" so that project teams can become self-sufficient.

- **Community Services**—Design and build content, such as common reports and data packages, for use by the broader business communities.

- **Communication and Evangelism**—Communicate and promote the status, progress, accomplishments, and successes, and chart the overall roadmap to the business at large.

- **Enterprise Architecture**—Direct, build, and support the technical infrastructure.

- **Education and Support**—Train and educate the business or related IT functions for the best utilization of the technologies it supports.

- **IT Governance Alignment**—Plug into the broader IT governance processes and steering committees. These areas can include project and change management, portfolio management, vendor management, and license management.

- **Data Governance Alignment**—Create a suitable framework for, or interface to, existing data governance disciplines across the organization.

- **Business Strategy Alignment**—Connect to the corporate business strategy. This ensures that the technology-related initiatives will meet the most important needs and priorities of the business. It helps define the longer-term strategic goals of the organization.

The functions of the BICC may also include:

- **IT Relationship Management**—Interact with and influence various other IT domains (e.g., data warehouse, database, portals, desktop tools, and ETL tools).

- **Vendor Relationship and Product Management**—Maintain constant contact with the BI vendors to understand and influence roadmaps/enhancements, make the vendor aware of challenges, recognize when the vendor strategy isn't aligning with your own, and so on.

- **Analyst Interaction and Market Research**—Be aware of emerging technologies, vendor health, and the like.

As you prepare your organizational and behavioral strategy, to help determine where and how your BICC is best structured, consider the following areas to take a pragmatic approach to forming and managing the growth within your organization:

- Where is executive support the strongest?
- Who is best positioned to help interlock the various business units and IT?
- Who are the stakeholders that need to be involved?

Remember, the BICC becomes most effective when there is a recognized need for BI that crosses functional boundaries. But to succeed, as we've mentioned, this BI requirement shouldn't be a strictly IT-driven initiative. The business needs to be actively involved in the creation and operation of the BICC. We look to the functional areas of business to empower our BICCs:

- Business users
- Analysts
- Power users
- IT support teams

Of course, their specific needs will vary according to their areas of expertise, but those who are facing the greatest challenges should be the primary candidates for creating the BICC. They can help form the initial community and become the guiding team to drive the first steps to success.

Key Concept

Developing the Scope of the BICC

As mentioned, our findings, working within our own organizations, indicate that the BICC's design will be influenced by business culture, historical deployment activity, specific business pain, and measures of success.

We've found we initially started servicing the business based on a smaller scope of tactical technical aspects of a BICC, such as support and consulting or project startup assistance. And then, over time, we've evolved our BICC models and expanded the scope by having the BICC play a far greater strategic and proactive role in our organizations.

BICC Roles and Personnel

We feel you should have a solid appreciation of the skills required to support your endeavor. The right selection of people and appropriate skills is paramount to the success of your BICC. The most successful BICCs maintain a mix of skills in which individuals—either in and of themselves or as the sum of all parts— manage the balance between technical and business acumen. The mandate of your BICC will determine which skills, roles, and staffing requirements are needed. As your BICC matures and the scope of its function diversifies, additions and changes to the roles and skills may be required to meet the service and capacity needs of your organization.

As an absolute minimum, we believe a BICC should consist of the following basic roles:

- BICC director/manager
- Business analyst
- Technical consultants
- Educators/evangelists
- Technology analysts (e.g., R&D on emerging technologies, roadmap awareness)
- Formal relationship managers with sourcing, IT infrastructure, and architecture teams

Realize that the people you appoint as participants in the BICC (fixed or virtual) may require additional and ongoing education and certifications to obtain the competency required to service the functions of the BICC, and these requirements will change over time as the overall requirements of the organization change. We think it's important that you clearly define the responsibilities of these roles, including the functions of the steering committee, leadership qualities for the BICC director/manager, and core roles and traditional responsibilities of the BICC team personnel.

Funding Models

One of the more interesting issues that our organizations have had to face is identifying the mechanisms by which the BICCs are funded. Each of us has had slightly different experiences with funding models, but the variety of experiences that we've had may be useful to your organization.

Most organizations understand the three easiest funding models:

- Self-Funded
- Shared Service Chargeback
- Centrally Funded Central Service

Self-funded BICC models are those by which an IT or BI department funds its own BICC activities. They may or may not engage or interact with others to start sharing best practices, infrastructure, space, licenses, skills, and so on. We sometimes refer to this model as *Early Stage BICC Funding*. There are, of course, pros and cons in this model.

- Pros
  - » Flexible
  - » Agile

- Cons
  - » Not revenue-generating, therefore not a sustainable strategy
  - » No connection between the different business strategies and the metrics that are developed
  - » Many people duplicating the BI effort
  - » Skills not leveraged

BICC *Shared Service Chargeback* models are those in which a central infrastructure is put in place, but there is a charge for every department that wants to join a project. The charge is assessed by the level of work required (does it involve consulting? do they want project startup help?), with a monthly fee associated for their usage on the system.

- Pros
  - » Reduces redundancy of resources in BI projects
  - » Connects data and reduces silos
  - » Creates standards
  - » Improves implementation timelines
  - » Creates efficiency when value for money is continually assessed

- Cons
  - » Departmental charges are sometimes onerous
  - » Early adopters may contribute more than "fair" share
  - » Conflicts may develop between corporate objectives and project objectives
  - » Investments need to be justified every time there is an upgrade or a new technology added
  - » Requires a level of record-keeping that may not be immediately available

The *Centrally Funded Central Service* model is employed when the charges for infrastructure, human resources, and so on come off the top of a corporate budget for use by all business areas so that organizations feel like this service is "free."

- Pros
  - » User adoption increases
  - » Skills are leveraged
  - » Overall business value is more readily realized

- Cons
  - » Less agile in introducing new technologies

Our experiences show that the BICC—by its very nature as an enterprise-wide service—will often require an organic and flexible funding model that is something of a hybrid of any or all of the above models.

For instance, in one of our organizations, the BICC is viewed as a shared service that any decision area in the company can use for free. It's funded at the corporate level. But there's a fine line that's drawn when a project moves beyond the advisory mode. As long as the BICC doesn't implement specific projects in the organization, its cost is hidden in the overall corporate budget as operating cost. But if the BICC is asked to take on development of a project, it will charge back to the specific decision area for hours and expenses.

At another organization, the funding model is even more nuanced. The BICC is funded out of IT overhead for a certain level of the headcount. Then, as the BICC personnel engage with specific projects, they bill their hours and expenses to the project itself. An initial engagement scopes out and estimates the development work, a draft of a customer service agreement is created to identify the start and end of the engagement, and the BICC quantifies the overall resources that will be required.

These nuanced, hybrid funding mechanisms represent where our organizations may be at the present time, but we acknowledge that evolutionary changes impact our models as our BICCs mature. For instance, in one of our organizations, less emphasis is now being placed upon direct billing. Instead, the BICC is moving toward the Centrally Funded Central Service model, which is reducing the requirements of direct billing to any particular decision area affected.

The point is that the way the BICC is funded reflects how the larger corporation has evolved in its appreciation of the benefits of a central BI strategy and how the successes of BICC initiatives and activities have been proven. It is important for senior management to recognize that the BICC is the face to the business and that strategic investment in platform, licenses, and resources to make the BICC effective is paramount.

Strategically Position the Organization for the BICC

Is your organization ready for a BICC? What is the state of your BI infrastructure? How can you recognize the current state of your organization? An important first step is to review your organization's perception of the BICC and the maturity level of the effort.

Maturity of a BICC

As the BICC matures, its needs, responsibilities, and personnel may change. We've also found that the BICC model varies depending on the needs of the organization as well as its level of maturity. It may be highly focused in IT as a means to help consolidate the system knowledge necessary to ensure a consistent enterprise strategy for BI. Other models may be focused in finance, operations, or a specific business unit, but all include key members of functional business areas and executive sponsors working closely with the IT teams. Some BICCs centralize at a corporate head office, while others are networks of regional and divisional IT and business stakeholders.

Whatever the configuration, the goal is to create a centralized, consistent approach to implement, support, and manage BI. This can ensure a successful deployment and broader usage across the enterprise so that BI is predictable, repeatable, and consistent.

> "Typically, you establish a BICC and supporting organizational structure as you are formalizing your BI standards and goals," says **Kay Van De Vanter**. "You wouldn't set up a BICC and then try to support every BI and Performance Management tool within your organization. You need to have a preferred or focused set of tools and an initial BI strategy with goals and objectives. BI may be fun and flashy, but this is a lot of hard work, and you need goals and objectives that your team can get behind and believe in."

User Adoption[8]

It doesn't take long for companies involved in the process of implementing a BICC to recognize that a key measure of success is the increase in user adoption, in both the number and the diversity of users across the organization. Putting BI into the hands of people isn't enough. It's not always the case that you can "build it and they will come." We've found it's essential to ensure that the technology is accepted and used effectively, and this requires that the BICC identify best practices and develop guidelines for successful implementation of BI tools. Below are five BICC success factors for attaining user adoption.

Success Factor 1: Creating Technology Standards

We've found that in the past BI was typically implemented on a project-by-project basis in response to specific user needs, with little attention paid to projects in other areas. In many cases, BI was acquired incidentally through other business applications. This invariably created a patchwork of applications that are difficult and expensive to maintain and support. The overlapping functionality becomes an increasingly common problem in large organizations, and the existence of multiple disconnected BI projects leads to higher procurement costs, greater training expense, longer project implementation, and information inconsistency. This is usually the case if an initiative is realizing little value.

But creating standards and broadening adoption is a strategic process. It's one of the areas where all organizations have had struggles and where the varied desires of business users come into frequent conflict with technology teams within IT. Still, standardization can bring considerable direct and indirect return on investment (ROI). Here's how that ROI can be achieved:

- **Direct Benefits**
  - » **Reduced Project Costs**—With a repeatable approach, new BI projects can be implemented faster, on time and on budget, with less rework and fewer cost overruns.
  - » **Reduced Technical Infrastructure Costs**—With a standard BI architecture, multiple projects share technical components, resulting in less duplication, less need to prototype alternative solutions, and lower training costs. SLAs are also improved.
  - » **Greater Leverage with Vendors**—Having standards increases the business leverage with the retained suppliers.

- **Indirect Benefits**
  - » **Higher End-User Acceptance**—Having a consistent look and feel across different applications and clear help desk and training policies helps to increase end-user acceptance and use of the solution.
  - » **Greater IT Satisfaction**—IT teams have more time to focus on the customer delivery aspects of projects and on high-level architecture issues.
  - » **Better Use of BI**—A standard approach can provide increased access to relevant and timely data, which enables a more complete view, extending the value and use of information in an organization.
  - » **Improved Use of Resources' Work/Life Balance**—As projects become easier to execute and support via standardized platforms and

practices, reducing the amount of "emergencies" and "rework," more time can be spent on new work and innovation.

» **Improved Delivery**—Through improved use of technology tools tailored to BI and established practices and processes, delivery is accelerated.

Success Factor 2: Converging IT and Business Users

To build BI implementations that the organization needs and users want, the BICC should be a partnership with the business users and IT to form individual BI project strategies, determine information requirements, and work out issues. This will ensure IT delivers relevant solutions that more users will want to use.

Getting the subject matter experts from the business side involved is extremely important since it's their lives you're affecting. If you don't get them on board, their reluctant adoption of the projects will be telling.

How to get business users on your side? Solve their pain! Seek out champions on the business side that understand the value you can bring to them. We've all seen how gaining an early, high-value win was vital to the larger successes that followed. It helps to build positive momentum throughout the organization and further the goals of the BICC strategy.

Success Factor 3: Providing Accessibility

You can't establish a standard and then make it difficult for people to comply with it. Timing is everything, so getting people on board quickly is critical. Otherwise, you can lose your users.

Some strategies and proven practices in this area include these:

- **Free or Low-Cost Access and Entry**—Provide "free" access, at least on a trial basis. If users perceive that the software is both available and "free" (or very low-cost), IT can gain significant buy-in. The best strategy is to have IT cover the software as overhead in an existing infrastructure regionally deployed. It will increase adoption and establish alignment to the standard.

- **Self-Service**—Find the right balance of self-service and IT support. We've found that often a self-service tool can mean fewer headaches and less time-consuming support for the BI team. If users don't have to wait for the BI team to create cubes or build reports for them, they can begin using the tool to achieve what's needed and fall into alignment with the standards sooner.

> "People want immediate gratification. For a strategic BI initiative, you can't expect people to wait three years to realize value," says **John Boyer**. "You have to plan the interim solution. How do people do business for the next six months? When people are not provided interim solutions, they will seek the path of least resistance. To increase success, walk before you run. Align your goals in the interim, and then merge into the roadmap when it's time."

- **Enterprise Licenses**—In many cases, it's a good idea to go with a vendor that offers an enterprise licensing model. This model can be managed centrally and provides for scalability as the organization grows or needs to expand. An enterprise agreement helps in standards enforcement (e.g., no negotiation on a project-by-project basis, no budget issues). From the business users' perspective, this eliminates an immediate barrier of needing budget and resources to implement it, and they can get up and running more quickly at a lower cost of entry.

- **Enterprise Architecture**—With an easily expandable platform offering, ramp-up time is reduced; procurement discussions are mostly about capacity planning; support services are leveraged; consistent release management is offered; and services are more easily managed, upgraded, and aligned with other IT component strategies (e.g., database upgrades). This also enables an excellent view of the BI ecosystem and enterprise metrics on performance, usage, and the like.

Success Factor 4: Providing Product Management

It is important to have a single point of contact for managing the BI standard, training, vendor relations, support, and issues resolution. This way, there is no confusion for users or IT teams, and there are far fewer redundancies. In most cases, the product management contact should be someone with a technical focus, rather than a business focus, but who will work closely with the business to ensure that requirements are met.

Of course, providing a structure for user training is a key requirement, and we'll go into that in more detail later in this chapter.

Success Factor 5: Ensuring Timely, Trusted Information

If users do not understand and trust the data, they will not use the solution. Providing timely information and confidence in that information—trust, understanding, and the proper reach to the information silos—will also increase adoption. Many teams will implement BI on an array of data silos without understanding how the information is connected or what information is needed to realize value. And these information silos may have low-quality data that is not trusted or understood. Or a business user may have to wait too long for requested information, thereby hindering adoption.

To achieve timely, trusted information, a strong partnership between IT and the business units is needed—with a business alignment strategy to ensure the goals are achieved as well as a partnership to ensure the information is high-quality, trusted, and understood.

Communication

If the organization clearly understands the value and benefits of an enterprise-wide BICC initiative, more users will want to cooperate and learn about it.

Broadening the user base requires communication and information-sharing. It is essential that there is a strong communication strategy in place to spread the message of the importance of BI to everyone across the organization.

We believe supporting user groups or a community of practice—which provide a forum for people to demonstrate their solutions—is a particularly useful technique. The idea is to share as much information across the business as possible.

In the communication strategy, these elements should be considered:

- Provide a proof of concept.
- Invite your vendor to demonstrate the software.
- Showcase innovative solutions people have found while using the technology.

It is also important that the value of strategic BI is communicated, both in terms of how it connects to strategic goals from the business alignment strategy and how often it is used by the business. This ensures ongoing support, especially from upper management.

Key Concept

You will want to understand, gather, and document the major business benefits gained by the various business units using the solution. For example, is the accounting department able to close the books in hours instead of days? Were sales increased, or were marketing campaigns more effective? Also, a way to determine engagement could be by running usage reports on your BI—that is, documenting how many times a particular report is run, by whom, and how often it is opened. Regularly communicating key wins in the organization to the broader team will help to gain and maintain momentum for the initiative.

Once the organization understands the key metrics it needs to measure and monitor, the organization also needs to understand how it can better achieve results, what results have been seen to date, and how to document and communicate the value.

Showcasing

When deploying something as large-scale as BI, project champions and their teams should be prepared to use proof-of-concept successes and a variety of communications tactics to acquire the mandate and then get users progressively more involved throughout the execution phase.

Demonstrating the value proposition of your BI initiative through a marquee project and building on that success with other wins, communications tactics, demos, training, and recognition will help maintain high-level interest in BI and keep the whole company interested, engaged, and involved.

Getting executive buy-in for your BI initiative is absolutely key, but that support has to be sustained once achieved. Early buy-in must also snowball into broad user adoption during execution. The best way to keep the momentum going and get the troops on board is to showcase your BI initiative—communicate success and demonstrate value, and keep on doing it.

How to Demonstrate Value and Communicate Successes[9]

We believe the BICC needs to be able to build on small successes, and then supporters must sell the capabilities of the BI initiatives. We sell ourselves every day. The tightrope we walk is to avoid appearing as if we're selling technology or a product, rather than selling a solution. To help you walk that tightrope, here are some straightforward ways you can showcase BI to your organization and ramp up company interest to the next level.

But before you try any of these showcasing tactics, make sure you're speaking the right language. Keep in mind the audience you're trying to reach, and demonstrate the value of the initiative in the business terms they'll understand.

A Successful BI COP

At one organization, a grass-roots BI Community of Practice (COP) has been in existence for 10 years. A large group with global representation, the COP provides a forum for leveraging tactics, practicing development vendor presentations, marketing of solutions, and discussing strategy. This forum has led to leveraged solutions, vendor enhancements, shared services improvements, and the creation of a large network of practitioners. The community maintains a Web site, hosts annual meetings, facilitates vendor demos, collaborates on practices and solutions, and is a main point of contact for vendors and internal IT and business partners.

Select a Marquee Project and Publicize It

What pain did a BI project help to solve in your organization? Pick something that's not too complex (for example, a simplified process for aggregating sales results across a number of regions), and start telling the story through email campaigns, word of mouth, face-to-face meetings, and so on. Your marquee project will demonstrate that the value of BI far outweighs the change it requires.

Solicit and Share Other Success Stories

When that marquee project story gets a bit tired, identify other new projects you can talk about. Constantly be on the lookout for success stories, and share them widely.

Talk to the communications department about using existing platforms to get the BI message out. For example, regularly send out an email newsletter with user tips, success stories, news, and recognition. Pepper the intranet with BI FAQs, tips, a user blog, news, and other information. Hold regular lunch-and-learn sessions showcasing BI successes, tips and tricks, or business usability and adaptability.

Relate the Successes Back to Established Metrics

IT and business have partnered to understand the key metrics they need to measure and monitor. Now articulate that ROI to the whole organization by communicating your documented wins and sharing the major benefits various business units gained by using BI solutions. For example, maybe operations identified a critical issue in the supply chain and was able to resolve it before it impacted delivery. Or perhaps sales have increased or marketing campaigns have become more effective. Measure the value and demonstrate it.

Demonstrate Success

You can engage everyone by gathering people together often and showing them what the BICC can do for them. Live or interactive demos are almost always better than static feature lists. Use various media creatively to maximize exposure and involvement. Make sure you show some before-and-afters: What was the pain? How did BI solve it?

Lunch-and-learns, Webinars, BI user groups, and vendor-sponsored BI User Days are all great ways to demonstrate what BI is doing for your organization.

Train the Trainer

Training is one of the most organic ways to articulate and showcase the value of BI. A good place to start is by training and certifying business users willing to act as trainers, as they become the point people for sharing knowledge and in-house training for general users. Next, train power users and flow major reports and analysis through them. Hold workshops every month to go through basics in areas such as analysis, score-carding, and reporting, and send individuals for vendor-held training when appropriate. Establish in-house or use external certification programs and publicize who has been certified.

Keep Management Involved

Those key executives who bought in early are going want to push the platform out to more users. It needn't be much more complicated than the CEO standing up in front of a crowd and endorsing the BI initiative. You can hardly get a better showcase than that. Make sure these individuals are talking about BI in their meetings or large departmental or corporate get-togethers and that they are armed with presentations, slides, and information ready to use when appropriate.

Go Viral

We've talked a lot about starting at the top and getting executive buy-in, but while you're at it, don't neglect the ranks further down. Use the early adopters and natural marketers in your organization to help spread the word on BI. For example, one company's IT department actually engaged the sales team to use its sales conference to talk up the great things IT was doing with BI.

Be Creative

Recognize innovators and early adopters, and encourage everyone else to get on board by having some fun with your BI initiative, while boosting morale at the same time. One company promoted its BI system with a week-long scavenger hunt. Each morning, they asked the contestants to find the answers to questions on the BI system, which got progressively harder as the week went on. The idea was to get users to explore the whole system and learn some of the more advanced aspects of it, while also learning how BI could help answer their own business questions. The game ended with an awards ceremony with management recognizing the best players and teams.

Be Progressive

Look forward. Don't be content with simply meeting today's business require-ments. Try to anticipate future requirements and growth. Each quarter, you should be able to demonstrate new capabilities, functions, and integration. Evalu-ate beta programs within the BICC so that your team can talk intelligently about future direction and roadmaps. Evaluate new and supplemental technologies.

Training

Having IT teams and business users who are unfamiliar with new technologies and systems is a major hindrance to adoption. Don't overlook individual prefer-ences and comforts when using technology. Often, individual users may feel embarrassed to let teams know they are not familiar with a technology, or if they do not have a lot of experience with a technology, they may not know what it can do or what value it will provide them.

A training plan is a major element of the organizational and behavioral strat-egy that is going to help drive adoption in an organization. And we believe organizations should maintain a training plan that matches user preferences to training types and needs. This will maximize the value of the solutions.

Recognizing that individuals also respond differently to the various types of training, you may wish to consider an array of training types to increase success as you build your organizational and behavioral strategy. Consider adding various types of training to your menu:

> "We find that by proactively planning, we can effectively introduce new technologies," says **Brian Green**. "We include funds for BI staff development in our budget. We also develop in-house training sessions for end users to ensure that the BI tools and technologies we deploy are appropriately utilized. We publish periodic newsletters and surveys to keep our user community informed and to provide feedback. The key is to plan and budget for mass communication and for training."

- **Public Classroom Training**—Public classroom training provides a high-engagement model of training in which users are free from the distractions of their everyday work. Hands-on labs, instructor-led training, and case study exercises can engage users in a way that will make them more productive with the tools and expand their knowledge.

- **Onsite Training**—Delivering onsite training for a group of users will also provide high engagement tailored to their area or business unit.

- **Conferences and Vendor Training**—By attending a conference or vendor-led training session, a group of users can experience the deep training necessary for their work, get a comprehensive understanding of the product and vendor strategy, and meet other individuals outside their organization who can help increase their success through knowledge-sharing and networking.

- **Online Training**—Due to travel constraints that may exist in times of economic downturns, online training can be a cost-effective way to improve the knowledge of your users. By also offering these sessions on-demand, you can provide the flexibility needed across various time zones and accommodate busy user schedules.

- **One-on-One Training**—One-on-one training is ideal when the skill gap is substantial and the user is a key individual in the organization who needs hands-on training. This may be the most effective training method, but it may be the most costly. Some project methodologies—agile, for one—allow the project manager to build in a certain amount of knowledge-sharing through pairing individuals on the team.

Communication in the Requirement and Design Process

Communication in a project starts with a good understanding of the requirements. One process that is important to establish early is the standardized recording of the BI prospects and requests for support.

This is clearly one of the opportunities where the BI team can bring together the evolving standards of the organization to align a proposed BI project with other ongoing projects and to bring aboard new decision areas with the overall business strategy.

> "One of the easiest quick-hit wins is cross-pollination," says **John Boyer**. "The BICC can be that bee that takes lessons learned in one project team to the next."

The standard requirements document should bridge both the business needs and the technical requirements. This means that it should be both transparent and easy to understand on the business side but still have enough detail on the technical implementation side so that real analysis of technical requirements can begin. Think of the process as the *conversation starter*: a standardized process that is easy for business users to embrace but critically detailed so that good communication is fostered between the business users and the technical staff.

> "The requirement and design process is iterative," says **Bill Frank**. "It's an educational process. It is a dialogue. You can't just ask and receive. Visualizing and understanding the data helps in the design process.
>
> "If you begin with a business goal and clear requirements as to what information is needed, there is a good understanding established. It has to be an ongoing conversation."

It begins with a documented requirement request, one that is not so many pages that it will deter the user from engaging. And what does a good requirements form look like? Well, we don't believe there is a "silver bullet" form, but we do believe there are many things the request should accomplish:

- The business outcome the user needs to achieve

- The information they believe is necessary to complete the request

- The dimensions and measures they need to understand

- The type of report they need to visualize

"We have developed a strong intake and management process for initiating new projects," says **Brian Green**. "Each request is submitted by business users through a workflow tool that routes the request to the appropriate team for a sizing estimate. The estimate then goes back to the business sponsor for review and approval. If an estimate exceeds a predefined threshold, the request will be escalated for higher-level approval. Projects are prioritized based on high-level business objectives and potential benefit to our customers.

"We also monitor ongoing projects through our corporate Project Management Office. We will often use an iterative approach at the outset of an initiative since business users cannot always visualize everything that can be accomplished with BI from the start. Through the use of prototypes and iterative development, we can ensure that our customers will be satisfied with the end product."

Knowledge Share

A centralized repository or intranet site can also help improve communication and understanding and provide a way for users throughout the organization to find the information they need themselves and feel empowered. This repository should be not only a repository for all the documentation needed to understand technical information, training, and best practices, but also a place for users across the organization to understand the value and celebrate successes. It can also provide a collaborative environment to share and discuss information. Including the plans, business cases, and documented wins against these plans will go a long way toward helping users understand and recognize the importance of the initiative.

Managing Change

Managing change in an organization is often one of the hardest tasks in the equation. Every change requires resources in place to support it. An effective communication plan has to be well-planned and communicated broadly. In many cases, project management or change management officers can provide guidance, so they should be engaged in this process. We have found that some effective strategies can make transition a lot easier:

- Consider all the possible derailment factors and plan for them in your organizational and behavioral strategy.

- Keep in mind that your organization's goal should be that every individual inherently *wants* to improve the business. Recognize that, while individual strategies may *seem* different, we are all trying to achieve the same goals. Be sure you are able to translate overall value into the departmental language.

- Remember that professionals don't like to be *told* what to do; they want to be *involved in the process*. A key to alignment is the carrot, not the stick.

- Measure and communicate success. Celebrating successes helps to build momentum and allows individuals to understand the results and feel the thrill of accomplishment.

Creating a structured approach to BI enables the ability to track and measure the multitudinous projects that make up a larger BI strategy in the organization. It permits strong communication between the various stakeholders and ensures that best practices are maintained in the process. With a structured model in place, members of the team can discuss and prioritize the work that needs to be accomplished, while providing a common platform for normalizing the projects to achieve the maximum benefit to the organization.

Checklist of Recommended Approaches

☑ Learn and understand your unique business culture and how it affects your strategy. Engage others to assess where your political situations most often occur and why that might happen, and assess the ability to drive a culture of performance in your organization.

☑ Determine your key stakeholders and engage them. Understand who your biggest roadblocks are and who your biggest supporters are. Determine which executive stakeholders need to be engaged for your success and which executives are already on board who can help you champion the initiative.

☑ Create an organizational structure. Define goals, mission, scope, roles, and a funding model based on your unique business culture, current structure, and maturity level—and expect this to change over time. In addition to a structured and dedicated BI team, build a community of stakeholders. Determine whether some of your key roles can be done within or outside the structured team and embrace them.

☑ Study your user adoption. Understand and benchmark your current adoption to be able to measure success in the future. In addition to understanding the number of users and time spent on BI initiatives, also determine where your challenges lie to help you best identify where focus is needed to increase adoption.

☑ Design a communication strategy. Communication needs to be constant and consistent. And it involves consultation, not dictation. Determine which communications tactics to employ in your organization to showcase and celebrate success, share new practices, and provide open forums for discussion. Ensure contact information is front and center and that the various groups feel there is an open door for collaboration.

☑ Determine your training strategies. There are different levels of training that should be used depending on the type of role. Training should be continuous as new members join the initiative, as you include new solutions, and as changes to the initiative are made. A trained user is more likely to engage in the initiative and costs less to support.

☑ Determine the processes and vehicles you'll need to employ to help engage users and earn their trust and confidence. This includes processes to communicate requirements, determine priorities, make changes to systems, and share information. These processes should be built to engage users, not prepared in such a complex fashion that they will deter users from engaging.

Organizational and Behavioral Strategy Overview

Business Culture

Provide background on the existing business. Prepare a few words that demonstrate the culture (e.g., consultative, authoritarian, partnerships). In particular, describe the existing BI/IT and business relationship in the organization.

_____
_____
_____

Assessment

Assess the current situation. Do you have groups that are already working together? Are there formal or informal teams working successfully together? Are there teams not being serviced that are critical to success?

_____
_____
_____

Stakeholder Assessment

Describe who your business champions are by business area, listing particular individuals and their roles. Which individuals and departments do you consider to be roadblocks to the initiative? Which other stakeholders (e.g., information management, IT infrastructure) do you need to embrace?

_____
_____
_____

Executive Buy-in

Prepare a matrix of executive stakeholders. Explain their current engagement and knowledge level of the initiative. Rate the level of involvement (high, medium, or low) needed from each of them, and compare against the current involvement provided. Determine each executive's key objectives and the value this initiative will provide directly for that person (what's in it for me?). Give examples of success that can be used to engage each of them. Determine the "ask" that you have of them.

_____
_____
_____

Communication Plan

Prepare a communication plan for your stakeholder teams. How often will you meet live, and for what purpose? Will you provide newsletters and, if so, with what frequency? Describe how you will communicate success. How can you communicate value as it pertains to the various stakeholders? Are there company initiatives where you can provide news and updates? Viral methods? Regular teleconferences? Workshops? Are there executive meetings or key stakeholder meetings you can join? When and what will you present to each group, and in what timeframe? How will you solicit feedback?

_____
_____
_____

Organizational and Behavioral Strategy Overview

Organizational Plan

What is the proposed organizational structure that should exist? Is it virtual, structured, or a combination of both? What are the charter and mission? What are the goals and objectives? What is the business case for this investment, and what are the key IT efficiency, business efficiency, and business effectiveness metrics that can be applied to this structure? What functions and roles will it support, and how do you expect it to change and evolve over time? What is the funding model? What will you name the teams?

_____
_____
_____
_____

User Adoption and Enablement

How do you plan to manage user adoption? What is the expected growth (which can be measured according to your roadmap and business alignment strategy in partnership with the business teams)? Will you provide knowledge sharing? Ensure support is available? Prepare for project startup? Are there guidelines, processes, and handbooks you should supply to deliver the right information in a timely manner? How will teams determine who they can go to when they need assistance? How will you bring users and teams on-board? How will you provide accessibility and security?

_____
_____
_____
_____

Training Plan

What types of training (e.g., technical, data and information) are needed? Who will provide the training? What methods are needed to satisfy both on-site and remote users? Are there "train-the-trainer" opportunities?

_____
_____
_____
_____

Requirement and Design Processes

How will teams define requirements? Do you have design and testing processes in place? Are there templates or Web forms? If so, have these been tested with users to ensure they won't hinder adoption? Is the information designed so that users can understand the information they are looking for?

_____
_____
_____
_____

Organizational and Behavioral Strategy Overview

Knowledge Share

How will you enable knowledge sharing? Is there a Web portal that can easily help users access training, help desk, and project teams? Can they share best practices? Read documentation? Easily view roadmaps and plans? Are successes publicized?

_____

_____

_____

_____

Change Management

Is there a change management team you can engage? What timeline are you looking for to enable change? Are clear expectations communicated? Are they supported and understood by executives? Is enough time provided in different intervals to ensure ongoing success is visible? Are clear communication processes defined? How do you plan for future change (evaluating when change is needed and how often review should take place)?

_____

_____

_____

_____

Measuring Success

How will you benchmark over time, and measure against those benchmarks, to demonstrate success? What measures will you monitor to determine the success of your communication strategy, organizational structure, user adoption, training, buy-in, and other elements of organizational and behavioral strategy? How will you monitor and document these successes and further promote changes?

_____

_____

_____

_____

Chapter 3

Technology Strategy

In Chapter 1, we talked about how to align BI program initiatives with the overall business strategy and how an organization can create a roadmap of successes with prioritization that meets the needs and requirements of the business. In Chapter 2, we examined the embedded cultural and behavioral factors that influence change and the ways an organizational and behavioral strategy can be planned that will accelerate success and eliminate some of the most common challenges that arise in this area. To a large degree, these chapters only touched on the challenges of the IT infrastructure that enables a BI initiative. This chapter will now address the BI technologies and infrastructure strategy and focus on a number approaches we've found useful in attaining BI excellence.

Often, specifying the various components required for organizations of our sizes is a task fraught with complexities: each of our organizations is unique, and each has undergone a separate IT evolution. Each has embraced different solutions over time and learned somewhat different lessons in the process. So our task in describing a usable BI infrastructure will, of necessity, be to offer guidelines based upon our experiences. Yet the lessons we've learned can serve to inform your organization's BI infrastructure decisions.

For instance, we've learned—through experience and common sense—that our BI program strategy shouldn't be a monolithic, "one size fits all" line of attack: different users have different needs, and each user has a variety of differing requirements for accessibility and utilization.

We also know that building user confidence in the information system will be a keystone of our BI program approach, while performance, security, compliance, scalability, service, and uptime—among other things—will be benchmarks of our success or failure on the technology front. An agile BI initiative is required in order to meet the constant and changing demands of the wide range of users who need insight into their information.

At the same time, we need to be mindful of the costs as we seek to increase the return on investment (ROI). The goal is to help our organizations gain efficiencies and productivity. This requires us to architect a strategic roadmap by which we can chart the goals of our organizations as we leverage existing investments in the current infrastructure.

Finally, we need to measure our success, using metrics such as user adoption, customer satisfaction, ROI, total cost of ownership (TCO), the efficiencies created by being able to on-board and complete projects faster, the time savings achieved through the sharing of best practices, and the use of common resources and internal experts and dedicated product management support.

Like many organizations, our companies have invested heavily in information management and business intelligence. In most cases, the historical IT pathways our organizations followed weren't a single-threaded, straightforward, or simple road. In fact, the most cogent argument for establishing a new roadmap to BI excellence is to rid the organization of the technology scramble and cobbled-together solutions that IT has had to deal with as it struggled to meet business requirements. We believe that a comprehensive strategy will provide a measured, and measurable, path to achieve BI excellence.

In this chapter, we will explore the following questions:

- Why create standards or consolidate a BI infrastructure?

- How can we leverage existing IT technology investments supporting BI applications?

- How can IT ensure that the business has the best tools, supporting infrastructure, and proven practice to enable BI success?

- How can we implement a strategic, cost-effective BI infrastructure?

We provide our experiences to enable you to aim for these goals:

- A well-defined information infrastructure that can ensure consistent, high-quality information
- A trustworthy information base that supports the business strategy
- A well-architected decision platform to get the right information to the right people in the right way
- A series of best practices that can be shared across the company and break down the silos between IT, business, and business units

Standardization and Consolidation

Many organizations today are choosing standards in their BI, Performance Management, and information management tool set. Often, they are consolidating various projects to achieve higher levels of efficiency and to reduce costs. We believe that by choosing standards and consolidating our BI projects, we allow our organizations to more efficiently leverage investments in technology and lower costs while increasing ROI. Consolidation of BI initiatives permits us to develop a more cohesive view of the data and to obtain a common source of information and leverage solutions.

And while the financial reasons to choose standards for BI technologies are apparent—cutting costs, boosting revenue, and increasing profits—it appears that, just recently, standardization has become an initiative that many more organizations are undertaking.

Early BI adopters leveraged the power of BI in their first attempts to achieve a consistent view of data, but often these early attempts focused on specific

"Typically, a BICC is established around a set of BI standards," says **Kay Van De Vanter**. "You cannot be successful in your BICC if you have to support all BI tools available in the organization. You need to be able to focus on preferred tools and processes. You need to have a BI strategy in place with goals and objectives—a deployment roadmap. The BICC is not just the flashy new team that is put in place. It is there to support your BI strategy and standards. This is hard work. Also, having standards doesn't mean that the tools can't be from multiple vendors, but overlapping functionality should be limited and complementary, enabling the BICC to better support and be successful in deploying the BI strategy."

"Technology changes quickly, and the BICC must be in front of the curve and be aware of what their customers are looking for and at," says **Bill Frank**. "If we purchased everything every end user saw that they liked, there would never be a standard. It's important to educate both IT and the business about the current standard suites' capabilities, understand roadmaps, and continually assess gaps in the standards that might exist (and proactively look for candidates to fill the gaps). The BICC should have an 'R&D' component to maintain awareness and also provide the standard vendor's input on what their users need."

functional areas. Therefore, as multiple departments and divisions implemented their individual BI tools for their internal needs, they were likely pursuing their goals in different ways, using various technologies. Or, as in some of our organizations, different tools were acquired as our business grew through mergers and acquisitions, resulting in toolset fragmentation. But as organizations mature in their information infrastructures and gain the ability to use that information effectively for decision-making, and as they uncover new opportunities or gain the ability to act and react quickly to change, the strategic value of the information is realized. The ability to use the information with reporting, analysis, and other tools begins to create business impact, and growing this ability to leverage the existing data in new ways drives a BI vision.

Of course, to achieve effective use of this information, people in an organization use BI tools in different ways based on their job functions. It is recognized that the right tool is needed for the right use. Some need the ability to drill into detailed reports or conduct advanced analysis on a daily basis, while others need an at-a-glance view of overall performance. However, the implementation of different BI toolsets for various uses can produce confusing or differing results when a strategic vision is not in place. There may be a consistent view within one department but multiple views across the company. The result can be a reduced ability to focus on the outcome of the decisions that are being made and more emphasis on discussions about where and how the information was derived. And while empowering end users to access and use information is the desired outcome, without governance the use of BI tools can create data anarchy.

Fragmentation of BI toolsets in the organization also becomes a support nightmare for IT, while increasing both the cost to the organization and the complexity of the information. This fragmentation lessens the ability of the organization to gain visibility into its information sources and reinforces the information silos that exist throughout departments and divisions. The goal is to have a varied set of standard tools that are available throughout an organization to reduce toolset fragmentation in individual areas.

Creating a common set of standards for BI tools paves the way for BI to be both a tactical tool and a strategic resource. Our BI programs have established a broad set of standards across these tools, by which we can help to lead the organization toward its strategic goals in the use of technology.

Proven Practice

Choosing standards is more than merely an exercise in cost/ benefit equations. Several factors need to be considered, including how the tools interact and integrate with the various technologies that are empowered by the BI platform or the technologies on which the BI tools depend. Figure 3.1 provides a view of how an organization might implement a standard set of tools and the technologies that need to be considered in the strategy in which stakeholder alignment needs to be strong.

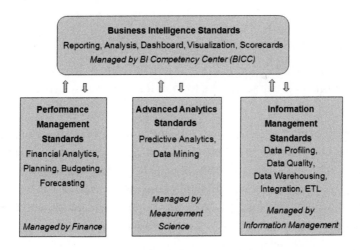

Figure 3.1: Sample standards management example.

In this example, the organization has created standards for each technology stack. The standards are managed by different groups, which interact with one another. The BI group also supports, consults with, and provides advice to the various teams about their standards choices. By establishing information and technology standards, our BI programs help to set the pace and ensure the resiliency by which the organization can meet its strategic information challenges. Some areas of our companies still retain specialized tools that were chosen to

"As Nielsen has grown and acquired other companies, we've collected quite a portfolio of technologies," says John Boyer. "We have had specific initiatives to define convergence and consolidation plans. The ultimate goal is to have a single technology in each domain. Our short-term objective is to sunset older technologies and map them to a long-term solution. The BICC is involved in evaluating new technologies and creating solutions for gaps that exist between requirements and the tool."

facilitate specific requirements. By evaluating those tools on an ongoing basis—both for fit within the portfolio of business needs and for future innovation—and placing those toolsets into a context of company-wide standards, we can help to guide and advise each sector in making better future decisions that will complement their internal goals yet connect with the larger corporate strategies. It is recognized that standardization does not occur overnight; it is a process over time. In the process, we're reducing costs as individual areas align to the standards, adding momentum and value to the BI effort.

Standardization Criteria

In its recent white paper, *Standardizing Business Intelligence*, Ventana Research identified a number of characteristics to look for when considering standardization[1]:

- **Broad Coverage**—A standard must meet the needs of as much of the organization as possible. This minimizes the exceptions that can lead to requests for non-standard technologies. In the BI realm, look for solutions that cover production reporting, planning and consolidations, ad hoc query, OLAP reporting and analysis, mining, dashboards, scorecards, visualization, and ability to support compliance with government and internal regulations.

- **Modern Service-Oriented Architectures (SOAs)**—Standards should leverage other standards when possible. Look for technologies that use Web Services standards such as SOAP, WSDL, and XML. These architectures will be easier to integrate with your existing environments and will be more adaptable as new technologies and standards evolve.

- **Scalability**—The underlying server technology must support the performance and scalability requirements of business users who expect fast responses to their business questions. Look for vendors that have distributed architectures where load balancing can be distributed across multiple servers. It is best if they can support multiple environments.

- **Heterogeneous Data Access**—Most organizations have many different data sources of many different types. Your BI standard should be able to access multiple heterogeneous data sources, including structured and non-structured data.

- **Global Capability**—A BI standard must be deployable in the language of the users' preference. Since most large companies have employees, customers, and suppliers all over the world, a BI solution must be multilingual and multi-currency-capable and be able to support diverse compliance requirements.

- **Security**—A BI standard should leverage and support your existing enterprise security. This means you don't have to duplicate or change the approach you've already implemented for information security.

> "It's important for a successful BI organization to be able to offer the 'right' tools to address the different needs of business intelligence users," says **Brian Green**. "There's an old adage that says, 'When the only tool you have is a hammer, everything is a nail.' Having a varied set of tools and solutions available through the BI organization helps reduce toolset fragmentation in individual departments and divisions."

Portal integration is also important to consider; the BI standard should be deployable in multiple portal technologies that might be in use in the company.

What Drives Consolidation

While creating standards around software tools reduces costs and boosts ROI, it alone can't achieve the goals of the BI program. As organizations grow, they accumulate layers of information resources. The goal of achieving a strategic platform of decision-support information may initially have been high on the priority list of the organization when transactional systems were implemented, but it often becomes a secondary requirement as the actual systems are implemented.

Consolidating those sources into repositories that contain common datasets—data warehouses—is the common step toward deriving a single version of the company's state. But data warehouses themselves are often fragmented among silos based upon division-level or departmental requirements.

We feel the real goal for consolidation is to bring the individual BI initiatives themselves together to unite the BI development projects with the overall requirements of the organization. A successful BI initiative typically requires that a huge amount of effort be spent on data governance, including data quality, modeling, integration, and transformation. Even the best BI tool in the industry cannot overcome issues of poor data governance alone. By consolidating these efforts, an organization will achieve important goals:

> "When standard tools are not funded at an enterprise level, it can cause a disincentive to use the standards, making the adoption of the standard a difficult task to promote," says **Kay Van De Vanter**. "The renewal of non-standard software licenses and the maintenance of existing BI silos appears to the individual project as a less expensive alternative than revamping and moving everyone to a standard."

- Lower the total cost of ownership

- Allow users to spend less time reconciling data and more time analyzing information

- Improve information consistency through use of master data and metadata strategies and accompanying governance models, leading to better analytics

TCO is lowered by reducing the number of iterations of analysis that result in the decision-support metadata: by orchestrating the BI initiatives, the upfront cost is higher, but the number of projects in the portfolio will usually decrease. This helps to maximize the efficiency of personnel, increases the skill level across a broader set of users, opens the door for hardware and software consolidation, and offers the potential for a more robust and strategic solution.

The information resources that result from BI consolidation can be better attuned to the goals of the stakeholders if several complementary BI initiatives are addressed in the analysis phase. This is one of the great benefits of the strategic BI program: it delivers a package of requirements to IT that can be more standardized and more targeted to management's goals. However, it must be recognized that addressing multiple stakeholders in a common BI initiative is tricky, given that usually only one stakeholder is considered the project sponsor. Having the ability to address other stakeholder needs is often the result of both a well-defined BI strategy—with a business alignment strategy and an organizational and behavioral strategy to support the technology strategy—and strong top-down influence within the organization.

The final result can be an information base that is more consistent and more global to the corporation's requirements, while still serving the needs of the employees at the line-of-business level. We feel that analytics that result from a consolidated BI initiative will better represent the "common version of truth" that our stakeholders expect. This improved consistency also strengthens the users' confidence as they build their analytical models: it's less likely that departments or divisions will battle over the data if there is a defined common vision. Instead, more time will be expended doing the work of analysis itself as opposed to reconciling differing reports.

Finally, if done properly, consolidation can greatly assist the speed by which business decisions are made. Less time will be spent acquiring the data from the varying data warehouses within individual silos, departments, or divisions. Instead, the information will flow more readily upward, toward the top, streamlining the acquisition processes and forming a solid, common platform upon which our decision-makers operate. Indeed, a well-developed data warehouse can be used as a source to develop marts to support business requirements.

> "In our recent BI Excellence study, 65 percent of survey participants indicated they were consolidating their BI and Performance Management systems within the next six months to five years," says **Tracy Harris**. "In addition, 48 percent of organizations indicated they had already begun this process or already had enterprise-wide practices in this area."

Matching User Roles and Capabilities

We believe a well-architected IT infrastructure must support the real-world analytic requirements of our users. Although an organization may have clean, consistent, timely data, if it doesn't have the right set of tools that users are comfortable with and/or it doesn't deploy the right methodologies to effectively access, analyze, and act on the data, then our BI infrastructure isn't doing its job.

Our organizations need a set of well-orchestrated information and analysis components that provide a completely defensible view of the business. This is what enables a company's ability to successfully compete and accurately forecast for the future. So we believe the requirements for a well-architected IT BI strategy should:

- **Support a Broad Set of Users**—Whether it's for the executives who expect an at-a-glance view at their desks or on the road or the business analysts who need to create complex analyses and drill deep into the data, the BI capabilities should be able to support diverse groups of users operating from a consistent information platform. That platform should be available, engaging, and usable so that decision-makers will want to work with the data. It needs to be available from anywhere, in the way users want and need it. The requirements of the various users must be taken into consideration: reporting, analysis, at-a-glance dashboards or scorecards, planning, advanced analytics, and other capabilities that are needed by a myriad of users.

> "I've seen problems when the business requirements are based on a previous solution," says **John Boyer**. "You can't force a technology into someone else's box. It will fail. When you are replacing a technology, revisit the business requirements from scratch. It's a perfect opportunity to get closer to a better solution. Another problem that's easy to fall into when gathering the business requirements is 'solutioning.' Even when the requirements are 'It has to look exactly like X,' the question is 'Why?' What are the requirements behind it? If the users can be flexible with the business requirements—or at least the way it looks—you'll be much further ahead in the end."

- **Provide High Performance**—Complex, data-rich reports can often cause long wait times for users who expect timely results in a fraction of a second. And, as information volumes and users increase, BI teams need to plan for an infrastructure that can scale and continue to deliver high performance.

- **Enable Action**—Information is only as good as its ability to enable action. By delivering event alerts, ensuring information is timely and usable and linked to other technologies such as forecasting and planning, or allowing access to information when mobile or in real-time, you ensure that users can best act on the needs of the business in a timely way.

To achieve this kind of IT BI architecture, we must have a thorough understanding of the business dynamics *and* the cultural dynamics.

We can't stress enough that our aim is to deliver the right tools to the right people. Users need to access information according to their roles and business needs. It's absolutely clear to us that a monolithic, "one size fits all" approach cannot deliver these elements from the IT BI architecture. As a result, we are constantly tuning our IT infrastructure to provide the toolsets that deliver the best solutions within a context of standardization and consolidation. The technology strategy needs to plan for the right set of tools to satisfy the business requirements set out by the strategy and must continue to evaluate new capabilities throughout the program's lifecycle to continually meet the new demands of the organization.

> "The BI organization should have an ongoing R&D mission to review and evaluate new capabilities," says **Brian Green**. "This idea isn't always easy to sell, particularly in tough economic times. Nevertheless, planning for R&D as an ongoing effort reaps many rewards."

Gaining IT Efficiencies

We've already discussed some of the technical and financial advantages of standardization and consolidation in terms of reduced TCO and IT support. But we can take these thoughts a further step to identify how those advantages can be translated directly into IT efficiencies.

For instance, it is one thing to identify a set of requirements for standards and consolidation but quite another to identify how to accomplish those requirements in a comprehensive and structured manner. The task is particularly daunting for organizations that are large and/or are experiencing rapid growth through acquisition of new companies. As user communities grow, so too does the demand for more ways to interact with the information through dashboards, customized reports, and so on. These demands often result in the need for additional tools, training, and support.

But the proliferation of BI tools can quickly become an overwhelming burden for IT, which has too many tools to manage and too many requests to service. It can also become confusing for the business user: Which tools should be used? Whose numbers are trustworthy? Often, the result is that business users revert to old tools and spreadsheets out of a sense of frustration. Standardization also means that business processes have to change for people who are on non-standard tools or are using manual processes for their reporting. The initial costs to migrate to a standard platform can be daunting, and businesses might be reluctant to fund an initiative that causes them "pain." As we mentioned in Chapter 2, a strong leadership position, in both IT and the business, that is related to the long-term benefits is paramount to the success of BI standardization.

Fragmentation and Reversion

As the BI infrastructure of tools expands to meet the demands of users, it can accidently create a dynamic that erodes the ability of the business users to successfully implement those tools. Why? Because users will have their own preferences, their own past training experiences, and their own criteria for usability. If there are too many BI tools, they will balk at learning another skill. They may reach for the tool they know the best.

This dynamic then reduces the ROI of the BI tools and increases the TCO of the overall BI infrastructure. It results in diminishing returns, not only for IT but for the organization as a whole. Users end up reverting to spreadsheets, information becomes more fragmented, additional time is spent reconciling silos of information, and projects fail, raising costs for the entire organization.

This dynamic of "toolset fragmentation/tool reversion" causes many projects to fail, and these failures reduce the return on BI investments. As user populations stop using the tools provided by the BI strategy, the overall TCO for the IT infrastructure rises. This demonstrates why the various business stakeholders need to be involved in the process of choosing the standards and need a strong consultation process in the business alignment and organizational and behavioral strategy development. Many standards might be chosen through the original use by business departments; it's important to the success of the strategy to apply the appropriate structure around them.

"A lesson that we have learned is IT needs to be more efficient. Users are very good at cranking out information in a spreadsheet," says **Kay Van De Vanter**. "If they are directed to use the BI tools for all of the information they require and then they are informed that all the data is not available—and provided an estimate of six months or longer to acquire it—they walk away, find another solution, or build a spreadmart."

IT and business stakeholders need a clear perspective on this dynamic and the way it impacts the overall organization. IT is just one of several stakeholders in the BI framework that propels our organizations forward. If IT and the business can communicate how

BI adds value to the overall organization, they are well on their way to justifying the investments in a standard set of BI tools and processes.

Using the Business Value Hierarchy

As previously mentioned, the Business Value Hierarchy is a good model to use when developing the technology strategy for the BI program. This hierarchy can serve as a framework whereby the different levels of value at different levels of the organization are considered and the means by which we communicate those values is kept in mind.

The first level of that hierarchy, as noted in Chapter 1, is IT efficiency. IT efficiency focuses on improving cost structures and improving the processes around the IT business intelligence work activities.

But we can't simply focus on IT alone because IT is just one functional area within the organization. We have to look at business efficiency overall. And this specifically includes the opportunities to improve decision-making—opportunities that are made available by business intelligence.

Once we can articulate the benefit that these business uses are going to realize, we can start talking about business effectiveness, which is at the top of the hierarchy and really focuses in on what these improved decision-making capabilities accomplish in our organization's ability to achieve strategic goals and objectives.

The goals, for instance, might be improving net sales, decreasing cost structures, and increasing customer satisfaction. In other words, we have to remember and understand that the whole reason for deploying business intelligence is for *improving* and *enhancing* our organization's ability to achieve these larger goals and objectives. Therefore, as we spend our resources on addressing the problems of data and toolset fragmentation—through standardization and consolidation— we need to look at the larger picture, beyond the costs of individual tools and the silos of individual data warehouses. In other words, we have to aim for the goals of overall business effectiveness while we are struggling with the TCO and ROI issues within IT itself. This realization expands the framework by which IT measures BI TCO and extends it to a larger corporate framework.

A Larger TCO Framework

It's important to recognize that the fragmentation of BI toolsets creates a basic conundrum for TCO, and that conundrum is the *hidden costs* that impact every BI project the organization undertakes. IT often looks only at licensing fees in setting the benchmarks for TCO, but this is actually a relatively small component of the overall, long-term BI spend. In reality, an upfront spend for enterprise licensing may actually *reduce* costs by removing an analysis and negotiation phase from projects and may help promote the standard.

Key Concept

Many other bottom-line expenses are also associated with BI projects. For instance, on every project, significant costs are associated with hardware, software maintenance, internal and consulting labor, and the creation of processes and practices. Having to negotiate a licensing agreement on every project can be frustrating for both the IT department and the vendor and may even delay projects and make IT look "unorganized" to business partners. In the graph reproduced in Figure 3.2, software license fees represent only 20 percent of the three-year TCO related to the implementation of any BI project.

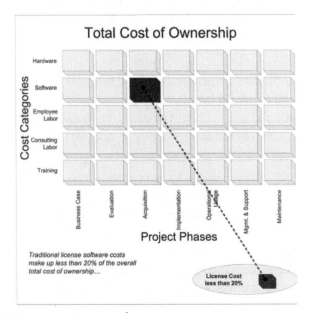

Figure 3.2: Total cost of ownership.[2]

As discussed in the IBM white paper *How to Reduce TCO and Increase ROI of Business Intelligence,*[3] we believe that if organizations can simplify, standardize, and consolidate the BI architecture using a better framework, IT can accomplish the following goals:

1. Reduce complexity of deploying BI and increase deployment agility

2. Cut the effort in meeting business requirements and deliver more efficient and effective BI projects

3. Save time managing the BI solution and reduce TCO

Leveraging Existing Investments

Some of us have had the experience—when discussing a consolidated BI infrastructure with the business users and IT—of justifying how the infrastructure relates to ERP or other application systems. For instance, a senior-level executive or an IT specialist might ask, "Why are you using a separate BI environment for this? Can't we do all of that through our ERP system?"

Indeed, many application suites (e.g., CRM, ERP, SCM) do offer modules that address wide varieties of information needs with application extensions designed to provide decision-support. And we often find ourselves using these modules to feed our data warehouses and BI environments.

There is absolutely nothing wrong with this approach, as long as everyone remembers that the particular underlying application system is probably transactional by design: it records and documents decisions made at the transaction level, and it may not have been designed for BI specifically. There is often a fair amount of confusion within the various application constituencies about the value of BI generally. The key is to communicate the larger vision of BI and to ensure that the politics of or preferences for any particular toolset don't overwhelm the goals of the BI infrastructure.

In our experience, particular IT areas or application suite constituents—those who are partial to one application—usually come on board when they comprehend the larger BI information issues. What they need to understand is that we're building the BI infrastructure to leverage the work they are accomplishing with their particular application suite.

So what are the arguments for leveraging existing application suites?

Leveraging Existing Suites

In our environments, the business models for the overall corporations—and the strategic planning associated with those models—often far exceed the limitations of the various application suites that have been deployed. While the tools are often good for line-of-business decision-support—for the particular user area or the division—they require quite a bit of configuration to become flexible and agile enough for the uses of the larger corporation.

> "We need to be aware of the 'ivory tower' views of separate groups that are managing architecture in case they get too far away from real needs," says **Kay Van De Vanter.**

Moreover, if our IT departments are supporting multiple application environments across multiple divisions (in some cases, even down to the lowest operational level), the complexity of maintenance becomes extreme and burdens IT with high levels of sustaining support costs. Meanwhile, the complexity slows the organization's ability to respond to changes in the overall business model. It also increases complexity at the transaction level and confuses the "consistent view" of the data across the larger organization.

We feel that the better overall solution is to architect a comprehensive Business Intelligence Information Platform—one that provides a common business model—that sits above the diverse divisions and transactional applications and reaches across the entire organization (Figure 3.3). This common business model is the official repository of the common view of data. It responds to the transactions that arrive from various solutions (e.g., CRM, ERP, SCM) but is not held captive by the processes that create the transactions.

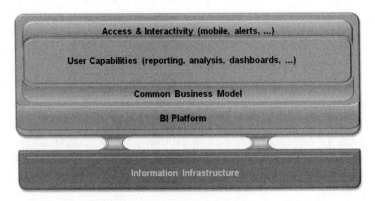

Figure 3.3: Business Intelligence Information Platform.

In other words, we want to actively leverage the transactional systems to feed our BI architecture and obtain a common business model. This leverage retains IT's—and the business communities'—ability to run the line-of-business applications by handing off the decision-support data to the BI Information Platform. This also permits the overall organization to build the upper-level decision-support environment without requiring lower-level decision areas to scrap or rebuild their transactional systems.

It's not necessary to try designing these models from scratch. Many excellent models and blueprints are available from both software and ERP vendors as well as independent or specialist data warehouse organizations.

Delivering the Information Platform

The goal of a "common view of the data"—the common business model—satisfies many of the information challenges in our BI systems.

Without this common repository of information—consistent among all decision areas—the difficulty in developing real performance management metrics becomes exceedingly problematic. On the other hand, achieving the architecture that connects the variety of systems together into a cohesive repository is equally daunting. The technical complexity is a monumental undertaking.

- How does IT ensure a complete view of all information in support of current and future business needs?

- How does IT build confidence in the data and ensure that everyone uses the same view of data across the organization?

- How does IT scale to support mission-critical deployments and minimize strain on IT?

- How does IT gain value from existing investments with the flexibility to respond to new business demands?

What we have learned in our experience is that a solid technical platform is required. Without it, it's difficult to ensure long-term success with a BI initiative. However, with the right information architecture in place, the solution can change and grow as the organization's needs evolve—including new capabilities, new users, new data sources, new technology environments—all without adding extra burden on IT.

Here are some of the elements of what we believe are key to this information platform:

- A platform that can reach all the information reliably and in a timely fashion with a roadmap that identifies all the data sources, not just the major transactional systems (when the BI platform is missing critical data, its use will decrease)

- A complete, consistent view of information in terms that business understands, owns, and trusts, which requires active involvement of the business to help define the terms and definitions

- A system management capability to confidently deploy, manage, and scale the infrastructure while achieving on-time service commitments

- An architecture that is flexible and resilient for integrating third-party solutions

Open Data Access

We believe that providing flexibility and optimized access to data is a key requirement of the architecture. We see the need for an architectural layer that sits above data sources and transactional application suites, enabling the transformation of the underlying data into the common business model (Figure 3.4). An open data access layer permits the underlying applications to feed the data into the model, using ETL, caching, or direct updates.

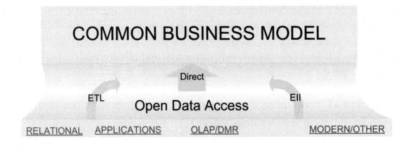

Figure 3.4: The Common Business Model with open data access.

There are a host of advantages in building the BI architecture in this manner:

- **Broad Information Reach**—Data professionals can gain access to data wherever it resides using published interfaces across transaction systems;

warehouses (relational and OLAP); flat, legacy, third-party integration tools; single query engine (SQL and MDX); or modern sources.

- **Flexible Data Sourcing**—Analysts have a choice of data-sourcing strategies—from ETL to Enterprise Information Integration (EII) to direct sourcing.

- **Single Query Service**—Data professionals can be assured of consistent and predictable queries across all data sources (OLAP and relational).

Consistent Business Information

Consistency in information is an issue for many organizations. Variations develop across the business through acquisitions, consolidation, and expansion. Business users need to be involved in defining a common set of definitions, business rules, and calculations across the business units. This daunting task can derail a common BI platform by delaying deployments and increasing costs as each area argues for its interpretation. This links back to the strong business alignment and organizational strategy in which an agreed-to roadmap and buy-in from the business is achieved. Organizations need to start with smaller subject areas that have more consistency across divisions. Showing off their success and capabilities to sell it to the next subject area for implementation is critical. We have seen that the "big bang" theory for this activity takes too long and usually fails.

However, if done correctly in a series of successes over time, this approach enables the following advantages:

- **Consistent Information**—Providing information users will be able to trust in order to adopt the solution. Consistency ensures everyone in the organization is working with the same information across all BI capabilities.

- **Common Business Model**—Data modelers can apply consistent business rules, dimensions, and calculations to data, regardless of its source.

- **Model Once, Package for Many**—Data modelers can build one model and deliver information in digestible-sized subsets for specific user communities. The users receive only the information relevant to them and are not overwhelmed.

- **Data Security**—Security can apply to users or groups all the way down to granular row and column security. Data governance can be sustained.

Finally, data modelers can respond quickly to the varied business demands for specific views of data without compromising the enterprise IT model or making the user wait.

This architecture allows IT to iterate quickly to respond to one-off business demands. It also means IT can create combinations of data unique to the business need and ensure that the business continues to use the enterprise model as its source of information.

Information Governance

As our BI information infrastructures have matured, one of the critical tasks that our BI teams have supported has been information governance. The way information is governed in an organization is critical to the success of the BI program—whether the BI team is actively involved in the governance process or is supporting the information governance team.

> "Data governance is an important but oft-overlooked pillar of the BI strategy," says **Bill Frank**. "People may not realize how important data governance (including the establishment of items such as metadata and semantics) is to the entire project. 'What is this?' 'How is this calculated?' 'What are the objects in my solution? 'Where are they coming from?' Answering these questions is one key to creating business confidence in the information."

With the silos of data that exist in organizations, there is often little cross-functional collaboration. Many organizations do not have formalized information governance and stewardship structures, with defined roles and responsibilities that we believe are critical to a BI infrastructure. There is a high price to improperly governed data: it can lead to bad decisions, missed opportunities, and increased risk for an organization. In many organizations today, governance programs tend to focus on the IT side of the governance equation rather than on the way the business manages its information (e.g., the ERP system sent 250K records and the data warehouse received 250K records). In addition, many decisions are made on data outside the sanctioned systems (such as employee-maintained databases, spreadmarts, or non-authoritative systems). Many systems have duplicate, stale, and inconsistent data, and there are few policies established to manage the information. And, when controls *are* put on the information, they are often counter-productive to the business needs, creating a cycle for more non-authoritative systems being produced in the business.

And while pockets of governance excellence may exist within organizations, there is typically no enterprise-wide approach. However, a proper information governance strategy can provide rigor and discipline to the process of managing, using, improving, and protecting organizational information. The information governance team needs to be brought into the equation to ensure the success of the BI initiative. Whether the BI program helps to support or manage the information governance initiative, alignment and a strong partnership with those who manage these processes is critical.

> "It is desirable to establish a formal data governance team with well-established roles and responsibilities using Six Sigma processes," says **Bill Frank**. "This will span business content and IT content encompassing master, dimensional, and metadata. Similar struggles occur in technology standards and architecture governance. Governance is always evolving and is a key to success. Without governance across all components of the BI, there is a risk of failure to the entire BI program."

Gaining Confidence in Information

Yet another key challenge in the development of the technology infrastructure in relation to the information management is in the confidence in the information that is provided. While that is a core component of information governance overall, the inability to access, trust, or understand information may not only disrupt the decision-making process but also hinder overall user adoption of a BI initiative. How many times is the BI tool blamed for the information it uncovers in the organization? This again demonstrates the importance of critical alignment between the business suppliers of the information and the teams that manage and govern that information. And an organization can consolidate its information infrastructures only if users have bought into the strategy and aligned with confidence.

If users fully understand the meaning, the source, and the context of the information within a given report or analysis and they trust the numbers they see, they will use that information to make business decisions.

From our perspective, improving confidence in the data is crucial not only to the success of our BI and performance management investments, but to the success of our overall organization. This is where metadata becomes invaluable. Metadata tools must be integrated into the overall BI architecture. Many vendors support this capability, and some provide the ability for end users to manage or contribute to metadata management. These are important considerations that IT teams tend to overlook when selecting a tool.

As mentioned in the IBM white paper *Improving Confidence by Increasing Understanding in Information*,[4] providing business confidence in information often relies on the following three areas:

- **Understanding**—Users need to understand what the data means and where it came from in their reports and analysis. This usually involves understanding the definitions around the data and the lineage of where it came from.

- **Trust**—Users need to be confident that the information is correct and can be trusted. This usually involves data integration capabilities such as profiling, cleansing, and de-duplication.

- **Relevance**—Users need unencumbered access to data based on security entitlements. They need to be able to quickly gather all the information that is relevant to their view of the world. Dimension management is an example of a technology that can provide relevancy to users.

> "Shared stewardship between business and IT in these areas is vitally important," says **Brian Green**. "The business steward details how the data is used in specific business processes and decision-making, while IT has the responsibility of understanding how that data can be properly integrated and optimized."

We believe that organizations with this baseline of data management maturity will get better value from their BI systems. They are also more likely to outperform organizations less mature in data management. So building confidence is a key requirement for our BI initiatives.

Deployment Considerations

As our organizations have grown and embraced BI technologies, we've all been faced with the need for a variety of deployment options for our BI infrastructure. And, as the needs in our organizations have grown or as technology has changed, these decisions have had to be reviewed, evaluated, and considered in the technology strategy to ensure the business needs are met. Bringing those options into a strategic decision framework has been one of the most important tasks that our IT organizations have encountered, and their solutions—though varied and robust—have a number of things in common.

First of all, our organizations needed a BI platform that could be confidently deployed and would perform with predictability. Technical complexity of the BI tools and resource constraints within IT could potentially limit the ease and speed of our BI projects rollout, and unless the IT organization chooses deployment solutions that are resilient, future maintenance costs or change management complications could quickly soar.

We knew there were important potential issues that IT needed to consider: users without access, users with access to the wrong information, poor performance, random system crashes. All these potential issues could shake the confidence of the user community and destroy its willingness to adopt the BI systems.

These are some of the IT technical requirements that needed to be addressed:

- **Service-Level Agreements (SLAs)**—Some of our IT organizations had SLAs with the business side of the organization. This meant our IT organizations needed to know that they could trust the technology solution being deployed and that downtime and poor performance weren't going to negatively impact the users.

- **Change Management**—IT wanted a means to streamline the process of assessing the impact that future proposed changes might have, as well as a consistent way to introduce the change as upgrades became available.

- **Security Transparency**—IT wanted solutions that would meet the highest security standards and leverage existing security standards that were already in place.

- **Performance and Scalability**—IT wanted a BI system to meet rigorous scalability requirements, so that as the organization grew it would have a variety of future potential deployment options that could meet the needs of growth.

Deployment Paradigms

Of course, the technical requirements of our IT organizations have become an important part of our BI standard processes, and as various technology deployment paradigms have advanced, our responsibilities have been to become advisors to and partners with IT to resolve and chart direction.

At present, there are essentially four BI deployment paradigms available to organizations of our size and complexity (Figure 3.5). While some are more commonly used today, various options are available, including these:

- Enterprise software deployment

- Virtualization

- Optimized business system deployment

- Cloud computing

Let's examine what each of these paradigms offers to our organizations.

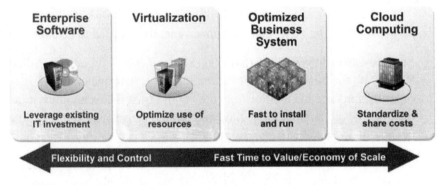

Figure 3.5: BI deployment paradigms.

Enterprise Software Deployment

The value of deploying the BI environment using our existing enterprise systems permits us to leverage our current IT infrastructure and mesh the deployment of BI with IT's current strategies. It permits IT to plan for future expansion and cost-effectively scale the deployment as our user communities grow. It's the natural first level of deployment for our organizations, as IT is able to integrate the BI platform with the existing heterogeneous hardware platforms, security, portals, and Web environments.

Most of our organizations have started out with precisely this paradigm of deployment.

Virtualization

Our organizations are well aware of the value of virtualization: it holds the promise of scalability, flexibility, and improved systems management as our user communities grow. And the opportunity to lower capital requirements and costs has been alluring. Some of our organizations are still in the evaluation phases in considering virtualization technologies, and some of our IT organizations have begun making modest investments.

Optimized Business System

Another BI deployment option is the optimized business system, which delivers packaged BI components on a preconfigured hardware platform. Optimized business systems promise to accelerate the deployment of the BI solutions with a "turnkey" kind of environment that doesn't require high levels of IT expertise. This paradigm offers flexibility and extensibility for analytics software, as well as adaptability to meet initial requirements while positioning for future growth in data and users.

Cloud Computing

The final deployment paradigm that some organizations are considering is the cloud. This option places the BI applications on a shared network across the enterprise. It lowers the cost and increases the productivity by provisioning BI as a service while maintaining corporate governance and control.

Choosing the Right Deployment Option

How an organization chooses a BI deployment option is a reflection of IT's long-term strategy balanced against the immediate needs of the organization to pursue a BI agenda. Table 3.1 summarizes the pros and cons associated with each option.

Table 3.1: Comparison of Deployment Options		
Deployment Option	**Pros**	**Cons**
Enterprise software deployment	• Flexibility • Integration to existing services • Control	• Longer initial implementation • Potentially less resilient to immediate change
Virtualization	• Maximized resources • Reduced costs	• Technical requirements • Customized environments (e.g., not possible)
Optimized business system	• Quick deployment • Controlled ROI	• Less flexible than enterprise software or virtualization options
Cloud computing	• Lower cost • Increased productivity	• Increased risk of security exposure • Limited integration

The deployment option that is right for your organization may also depend on your organization's level of maturity and the complexity of the environment you currently support—and it could change over time. In addition, an organization may choose a mix of deployment options depending on the use, such as a sandbox environment in the cloud with the production environment on the enterprise deployment. The most important advice we can offer is to position the BI infrastructure so that future deployment choices are not limited. Deployment paradigm options are important to ensure that the investment in the BI architecture does not become bottlenecked in a technology with a limited future. At the same time, options that meet the specific strategic needs of the corporation today but are flexible to the changing technological landscape of tomorrow, will provide an excellent IT investment strategy for years to come.

"With each deployment type, there are challenges that need to be understood," says **John Boyer**. "For example, when moving to a virtualized environment, you may first evaluate the capacity you need by checking existing hardware utilization. Don't make the mistake of looking only at the average CPU usage of the existing boxes and size from that. It is likely that the average CPU usage does not take into consideration usage spikes. You need to know the maximum CPU usage of the existing boxes, too, in order to plan the virtual environment appropriately."

Processes for Change and Development

Technology changes can impact behavior and user adoption, and preparing for technology changes needs to be planned early in a technology strategy. While these processes need to be considered in the organizational and behavioral strategy, they also need to be revisited in the technology strategy. Consider the following points when planning a technology strategy:

Proven Practice

- **Implementation of Standards**—The "big bang" approach rarely works. Consider migrating and sunsetting technologies over time in planning with business partners. In addition, provide incentives to business areas to buy into the program—with corporate-funded license costs, support for standard systems, and services to help them on-board—so that the reasons to migrate to standards become more compelling.

- **Testing**—Ensuring that a technology, a new report, or a new upgrade is stable and delivers the right approach for business users is extremely important in order to achieve user adoption and buy-in. The trust of the project is at risk if an hourglass turns too long, a report delivers the wrong information, or a new technology produces errors.

- **Requirements**—Ensure that processes for new requests are in place and that teams can understand how to easily ask for the support they need. Processes that are too long, cumbersome, or ill-defined will deter users from engaging.

- **Roadmaps**—Ensuring that stakeholders understand and are consulted on short- and long-term vision is important. Be transparent in planning, and deliver lead times to teams before embarking on changes. Understanding the plan and vision are important to maintaining buy-in. A roadmap that delivers timing, expectations, and strong communication on the steps will help to engage the various partners that are needed.

Recognize that clear processes are key to a successful technology approach. Change can be difficult and can impact the ability to achieve the envisioned goals. Clear communication and planning will help to avoid many common pitfalls that are encountered in technology initiatives.

Delivering a Successful Technology Strategy

Technology delivers the innovation needed to improve business outcomes. However, delivering a technology strategy that meets the business needs can be complex and wrought with challenges. Business Intelligence is a technology that can touch every area of the business, and it is interconnected with various technologies that can hinder or improve its success.

A successful BI technology strategy needs to be broad and must have the ability to adapt and change over time as new innovations enter the market or as business needs change. During planning, consideration must be given to the various business stakeholders—and to the various IT stakeholders—who will help increase the success of the BI program.

By understanding the business alignment strategy that will help to effectively execute on the business goals as well as the organizational and behavioral strategy that is needed to improve stakeholder alignment, a technology strategy can be delivered to achieve BI excellence.

Checklist of Recommended Approaches

☑ Assess the current technology environment in your organization. See where success has already been achieved, and identify best practices that are already in place. Set goals for the information technology initiative and determine how it can be achieved in incremental successes.

☑ Determine the set of stakeholders that need to be involved in the initiative, the core technologies that are needed for BI, and the additional technologies that extend, leverage, or support the BI initiative. These typically include the core BI tools—reporting, analysis, dashboards, scorecards—as well as planning, financial performance management, advanced analytics, and information management tools that can help deliver success.

☑ Understand how your business alignment strategy affects the capabilities that are needed in your technology strategy; a technology is an enabler of the business and needs to support these requirements. Demonstrate how a set of standards and the consolidation of BI initiatives will provide value to the users—in terms they understand. Articulate the benefits in terms of IT efficiencies, business efficiencies, and business effectiveness.

☑ Define the standards in the various BI domains that will provide the broadest range of capabilities for your platform, recognizing that different tools are needed for different users. Consider the users who need to use the system and the ways they need to use it (what their jobs and roles are). Align and engage these user communities to help determine the standards.

☑ Plan how the BI platform can support the delivery of information to your users with the consistency of information as the key. Ensure that the needed information can be accessed in a consistent way. Consider how the platform can scale as user communities grow, how the right level of security can be applied, how it can remain open and agile, and how it will integrate with the technologies needed today and tomorrow.

☑ Understand the governance approaches that currently exist in the organization, and determine the role that the BI program can play. Engage your information governance specialists and support and align with those teams.

☑ Consider the various areas of information management that will affect user confidence in the information, and ensure that a strong partnership with those teams is created.

☑ Consider your deployment options to ensure you can meet future needs, and do not limit yourself for future ability to execute.

☑ Remain open in communication. Consult teams about the roadmap and vision, and remain transparent in that vision. Develop a process for managing upgrades and changes and rolling out new initiatives. Consider the ways that delivery of new information and technology changes can impact teams.

☑ Determine a plan to remain agile, to introduce new technologies, and to remain innovative and competitive with the solution. Recognize that constantly changing standards can fragment a successful program but that standards need to be continually evaluated over time to allow for innovation and growth.

Technology Strategy Overview

Standardization and Consolidation

Why are you considering standardization? What are the benefits (articulated in IT efficiencies, business efficiencies, and business effectiveness)?

_____
_____
_____

Standards Management

What team will manage the standard? What are your recommendations for the standards that the BI team will manage? Why is each standard recommended? What funding model will support the standards? What standards will the BI team support/advise/consult with (e.g., financial performance management, information management, advanced analytics)? What process will you have in place for evaluating standards and introducing new standards? How will you remain agile in delivering against the needs of the business?

_____
_____
_____

User Capabilities

Based on the business alignment strategy, which users require access to BI tools? What is the requirement based on the need, and what tools do they need based on their job role? What interactivity level is needed? Are there access needs to be met (e.g., Web-based, mobile, offline)?

_____
_____
_____

Total Cost of Ownership

How do you expect to improve total cost of ownership with the chosen solution? How can you improve efficiency and cost across technology choices—from a software license, hardware, services, training, consulting, and productivity perspective? How will you leverage existing investments? What additional value will be achieved for these existing investments?

_____
_____
_____

BI Platform

What requirements do you have for your BI platform? What information sources do you need to access? How do you plan to manage information? What requirements are there for security? What scalability and performance requirements will you have over time? How can you ensure agility in meeting the needs of the business?

_____
_____
_____

Technology Strategy Overview

Information Management

What information management technologies do you have in place? How will you provide confidence in information from an understanding, trust, and reach perspective? What warehousing strategy underpins your BI strategy? What teams are responsible for these areas, and how do you engage?

_____
_____
_____

Information Governance

What information governance initiatives are taking place in your organization? How will the BI strategy interact with and support these governance initiatives? What stakeholders and communication vehicles are in place to support these strategies?

_____
_____
_____

Deployment Options

What deployment options exist in your organization? What deployment options are being considered? How will you evaluate new deployment options as they become available? How can you anticipate future needs for additional infrastructure options as demand grows?

_____
_____
_____

Innovation

How do you plan to continually evolve your strategy as technology evolves? What mechanisms do you have in place to monitor new technology needs and changes? How can you test new innovations and evaluate their value? What is your roadmap over time to introduce new upgrades or solutions in the short and long term?

_____
_____
_____

Measuring Success

What benchmarks will you put in place over time to assess success? How will you measure success in terms of IT efficiency, business efficiency, and business effectiveness?

_____
_____
_____

Summary

The Journey to BI Excellence

E ach of us recognizes that our journey to achieve excellence in business intelligence is still progressing, and that we are still adapting to the unique challenges faced by our organizations. We see our journey not as a single-threaded path toward a monolithic solution but as a strategy that will evolve over time and change as technology changes. We need to remain agile and to change with the needs of the business. It is a strategic endeavor to enable our organizations to link strategy to execution—to find new opportunities, respond to change, and help make smarter decisions. With a clear vision and a well-thought-out approach, we can better meet the current and future needs of the organization as a whole.

By connecting BI more closely to the goals of the organization and aligning to the business strategy—thereby improving business effectiveness—we can help our teams work toward the goals that matter to the organization as a whole. That's where our *business alignment strategy* starts. Consistent alignment and integration of an organization's data, within the context of the business strategy, leverages the basic elements of data analysis into realistic business measurements and metrics—using KPIs, dashboards, and other such tools. These consistent metrics are the bricks that will help pave the way to new successes for the organization.

Interest starts to pick up incrementally after a series of initial wins in servicing the needs of a few key stakeholders. Inspiring enthusiasm for the larger goals of the organization and creating an organizational and behavioral approach that will improve collaboration and productivity can result in business efficiency.

> "Project teams must acknowledge that some decisions may need to be made for the greater good of the enterprise rather than benefiting a single project," says **John Boyer**. "This is especially true when attempting to converge multiple streams to a single technology."

While many areas that have separate silos of information might be executing pretty well on day-to-day strategies, many may be distracting from or aligning poorly with the goals of the larger organization and its long-term strategy. We've demonstrated, using what we call an *organizational and behavioral strategy*, how we've approached these problems. Although there may be differences with each of our approaches, there are also many common elements that we see as being effective. It starts with assessing the culture of the organization, identifying the political structure, understanding the perspectives of key stakeholders, and then seeking the ways and means to bring about the needed support.

Finding key stakeholders who want to champion the vision of a comprehensive BI system is clearly important. The creation of a competency center—called by many different names and existing in many different forms within our separate companies—can help define the mission, the goals, and the scope of the overall BI vision. It's a key mechanism in changing how our companies approach the issues and requirements of BI. This BICC—consisting of both IT and business users—charts the path and measures the progress along the path to BI excellence.

There are likely several people in your IT and business areas who truly understand how BI can make a difference, and it is important to assemble them in these informal or formal groups. If you are one of them, take a lead: set up meetings for vendors to showcase their offerings, for your internal teams to present their successes, and to reach out to senior management and executives. You may be surprised at how receptive they will be.

Finally, driving continual innovation and IT efficiencies through a comprehensive technology strategy that includes standards, consolidation, and governance can translate into better results with a lower total cost of ownership for the entire IT infrastructure and a better return on investment. Our processes of establishing standards aren't aimed at providing the "one size fits all" solution. Instead, using the collaborative approach of the BICC to study and devise desired standards, we approach each user request for particular tools or reports from an advisory perspective. Based on the organization's needs, we offer a span of standard capabilities that we feel will achieve the desired results at the most appropriate cost, delivering the greatest efficiency.

In other words, our IT technology strategy is not to replace all tools in one initiative, but to deliver the best possible information that is appropriate to our environments. As we work on this strategy, we're mindful of the modes of delivery that our various users require, and we try to position our infrastructure through a variety of deployment modalities. We also keep an active eye on the competitive horizon for new, innovative capabilities.

> "We find that the business requirements are constantly stretching the limits of technology," says **John Boyer**. "For example, in order to meet service-level objectives for performance to the end user, we have had to bring together the brightest minds across IT—in networking, database, BI, and security."

Our concept is to construct a *BI technology platform* that is representative of our organizations' needs—a platform that is broad enough to meet the challenges of our complex enterprises. As this platform matures and evolves, it is being guided by the collaboration of the members of both business and IT. This *technology strategy* doesn't presuppose IT domination in the decision-making; instead, it recognizes that there is both a demand side (business) and a supply side (IT) to the requirements of BI excellence. However, it is IT's responsibility to proactively communicate the capabilities and govern the use of the BI tools and platform.

A Framework for Choice

Working in our different enterprise-level organizations, across a variety of industries and market sectors, we have attempted to distill our real-world BI experiences into this strategy framework so that others might achieve similar BI successes. We've demonstrated the impact of three separate strategies to achieve excellence in BI:

- A business alignment strategy by which the goals of the organization are aligned with business priorities and delivered in high-value wins that link closely to business effectiveness

- An organizational and behavioral strategy by which the culture and behavior of the organization can be fine-tuned to increase business efficiencies

- A technology strategy that can deliver IT efficiencies with an infrastructure to enable the organization in its quest for BI excellence

We believe this BI excellence strategy framework, which is depicted in Figure S.1, describes the best chance of arriving at a destination where these increased levels of business value of BI can be achieved. The three tiers of strategy don't map only one-to-one to the three value drivers—they in fact deliver value across all three—but there is definitely a stronger link to each level of value with a specific strategy area and a framework that provides focus in a strategy exercise.

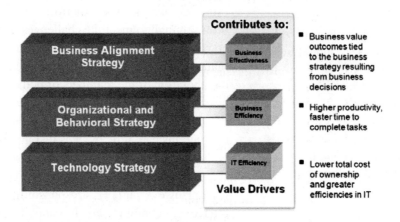

Figure S.1: BI excellence strategy framework.

We have also been able to put forward some proven practices and tactics and have provided lessons learned to enable a fast start to success. We offer all this as a potential blend of strategies and tactics that other organizations could replicate, adjust, and use at different times in their quest for BI excellence. It is obvious that while each organization should consider all three levels of strategy, there is no silver bullet or single road to success. What is right for your organization will depend on your existing level of maturity, culture, organizational structure, and vision. However, this book gives you the steps needed to craft a well-defined vision, with some solutions to overcome common challenges along the way.

Measuring Success

Measuring the success of the BI strategy is potentially one of the most critical takeaways of this book. If nothing else, remember that you need to continually benchmark your efforts to ensure you understand where you started and the success you have achieved in your program. Measure against the goals and the business case for each initiative to determine whether those goals are being reached. Document the organization's wins, and make sure they are compiled, archived, and publicized. We've learned that success measurement comes in many forms: business effectiveness, business efficiency, and IT efficiency. However, in addition to measuring the overall initiative or focused projects against the business value hierarchy, you need to measure each component of your strategy along the way. For example:

- BI Competency Center success

- Training and communication program effectiveness

- Business and IT alignment improvements

- Customer satisfaction with the program

- Technology innovation and architecture and infrastructure improvements (including licensing and service models)

- Cost structure improvement and a move from lagging to leading indicator-based analysis

Although this can be a time-consuming endeavor, it is one that is worthwhile. Understand that this is also not a one-time initiative but a continual process. As goals are adjusted and new requirements formed, you need to define and track new success measurements as well.

> "It's important to regularly publish updates to your strategy and measurements," says **Brian Green**. "Doing so will help to reinforce, in the minds of the larger organization, who is part of the BI organization and what it does."

The Future for BI Excellence

We believe that the current successes our companies are experiencing are linked to and supported by our business intelligence systems and the strategies that have enabled them. But we know that our tasks in BI are not finished. To be effective, they must continue to evolve.

Industry analysts predict that the future of BI technology will be an era in which our current systems must radically and rapidly adapt to an integrated global marketplace. These analysts believe this future is one in which the use of BI tools will be democratically expanded throughout the enterprise, empowering decision-makers at all levels of the organization. That is why a common view of the enterprise is becoming increasingly important. This requirement will continually spawn new and innovative tools that command this area over time.

How can we position our organizations to embrace such a future? Where will advances in technology lead us as information tools spread to every level and segment of society? How can our organizations respond to the changes and challenges of this evolving, intra-connected, highly personalized, and data-intensive global economy?

We are already seeing the convergence of BI, advanced analytics, performance management, and information management tools and strategies. We are also seeing social networking and collaboration being brought into the BI platform. Cloud computing, location intelligence, and new devices are all being watched by our teams to ensure we keep fresh with the changes to technologies that can be applied to a successful BI strategy. And each request by the business is evaluated to ensure that as we create standards and consistent BI platforms, we also evolve with the market and improve the technology infrastructure that powers business decisions.

We believe that by positioning our corporations with the strategies of BI excellence, evolving with the future is within reach. Instead of struggling to implement BI within individual silos and maintain parallel systems, our challenges will instead be to innovate upon a fundamental platform and expand the access points of our enterprise-level BI infrastructures. Instead of laboring to achieve consensus between business users and IT departments, our collaborative strategies will place us in the implementation lead, enabling us to embrace the new technologies in a structured, cost-effective, and profitable way. Moreover, as our management continues to demand better results, higher rates of efficiency, and more cost-effective solutions, we trust we'll be ready to meet those demands rapidly, vigorously, and with the backing of our user base.

That is, after all, the ultimate promise of BI excellence: to enable execution of a more effective business strategy with the right technology, people, and processes in place. We hope this book is a practical guide to your future with BI and that it helps you achieve a similar level of BI success and excellence.

Notes

Introduction

1. *The New Voice of the CIO*. Copyright IBM, 2009.

2. "IBM Cognos Study." *Computerworld*, March 2009.

3. *Pervasive Business Intelligence*. TDWI, 3rd Quarter, 2008.

4. Roland Mosimann, Patrick Mosimann, and Meg Dussault. *The Performance Manager*. Cognos, Inc., 2007.

5. Roland Mosimann, Patrick Mosimann, and Meg Dussault. *The Performance Manager*. Cognos, Inc., 2007.

Chapter 1

1. IBM Institute for Business Value. *Breaking Away with Business Analytics and Optimization*. Copyright IBM, November 2009.

2. "BI Excellence Study." Copyright IBM, September 2010.

3. Wikipedia, s.v. "Balanced scorecard," http://en.wikipedia.org/wiki/Balanced_scorecard (accessed September 7, 2010).

4. Wikipedia, s.v. "Six Sigma," http://en.wikipedia.org/wiki/Six_Sigma (accessed September 7, 2010).

5. Wikipedia, s.v. "Total quality management," http://en.wikipedia.org/wiki/Total_quality_management (accessed September 7, 2010).

6. "BI Excellence Study." Copyright IBM, September 2010.

7. Richard Connelly, Robin McNeill, and Roland Mosimann. *The Multidimensional Manager*. Cognos, Inc., 1997.

8. Roland Mosimann, Patrick Mosimann, and Meg Dussault. *The Performance Manager*. Cognos, Inc., 2007.

9. Roland Mosimann, Patrick Mosimann, and Meg Dussault. *The Performance Manager*. Cognos, Inc., 2007.

10. "Performance Management" presentation, Meg Dussault, October 2009.

11. "IBM Cognos Study." *Computerworld*, March 2009.

Chapter 2

1. Cindi Howson. *Successful BI Survey: Best Practices in Business Intelligence for Greater Business Impact*. BIScorecard, November 2009.

2. *Getting Executives on the BI Bandwagon*. Copyright IBM, May 2009.

3. *J18 – ROI Evaluation Report: IBM Cognos Software*. Nucleus Research, May 2009.

4. *Organization of Business Intelligence*. Business Applications Research Center, August 2008.

5. *Building a Business Intelligence Competency Center*, IBM, February 2009.

6. *Building a Business Intelligence Competency Center*. IBM, February 2009.

7. *Building a Business Intelligence Competency Center*. IBM, February 2009.

8. *Building a Business Intelligence Competency Center*. IBM, February 2009.

9. *Building a Business Intelligence Competency Center*. IBM, February 2009.

Chapter 3

1. Choosing a Standard for Business Intelligence: Simplify the IT Environment, Reduce Your TCO, and Increase Your ROI. Copyright IBM, January 2009.

2. Derek Lacks, "TCO Presentation." Copyright IBM, 2010.

3. *How to Reduce TCO and Increase ROI of Business Intelligence.* Copyright IBM, July 2010.

4. *Improving Confidence by Increasing Understanding in Information.* Copyright IBM, May 2008.